SO... WHAT DOES AN OUTSTANDING TEACHER DO?

What distinguishes an *Outstanding Teacher*? A question asked in numerous interviews – and one that's much easier to ask than to answer. Many teachers will admit they don't actually know what 'Outstanding' looks like. It's not about creating *jazz hand* lessons for a one-off observation through 'prepping, stressing, and box-ticking.' It isn't something that can be achieved in a single lesson. It is a craft that needs developing like any other skill. This guide expands on previous works by discussing long-term development, the benefits of embedding skills, learner attributes, and the impact of COVID.

Influenced by John Hattie's Visible Learning research, *So ... What does an Outstanding Teacher Do?* provides practical guidance and opportunities for self-reflection for teachers who want to maximise their positive impact on students' learning. Areas covered include:

- Feedback
- Student voice
- Self-regulation
- Teachers working collectively
- Differentiated learning objectives
- SOLO Taxonomy
- Questioning and observation

Chowdhary provides teachers with recommendations for enhancing practice that easily apply to any classroom, regardless of their subject, speciality, or position. Whether you are a PGCE student, an ECT, or a practising teacher, this book is a practical and accessible guide for any teacher who aspires to maximise their positive impact and become truly outstanding.

Cat Chowdhary is Head of English and Media Studies. She has ten years of experience working in the education sector, following the National Curriculum both in the UK and abroad. She is also a regular blogger on teaching and learning, particularly focusing on the work and research of John Hattie.

SO ... WHAT DOES AN OUTSTANDING TEACHER DO?

A Visible Learning Evidence-Based Approach

Cat Chowdhary

LONDON AND NEW YORK

Designed cover image: © Getty Images

First published 2023
by Routledge
4 Park Square, Milton Park, Abingdon, Oxon OX14 4RN

and by Routledge
605 Third Avenue, New York, NY 10158

Routledge is an imprint of the Taylor & Francis Group, an informa business

© 2023 Cat Chowdhary

The right of Cat Chowdhary to be identified as author of this work has been asserted in accordance with sections 77 and 78 of the Copyright, Designs and Patents Act 1988.

All rights reserved. No part of this book may be reprinted or reproduced or utilised in any form or by any electronic, mechanical, or other means, now known or hereafter invented, including photocopying and recording, or in any information storage or retrieval system, without permission in writing from the publishers.

Trademark notice: Product or corporate names may be trademarks or registered trademarks, and are used only for identification and explanation without intent to infringe.

British Library Cataloguing-in-Publication Data
A catalogue record for this book is available from the British Library

ISBN: 978-1-032-20622-6 (hbk)
ISBN: 978-1-032-20623-3 (pbk)
ISBN: 978-1-003-26445-3 (ebk)

DOI: 10.4324/9781003264453

Typeset in Interstate
by KnowledgeWorks Global Ltd.

DEDICATION

First and foremost, I want to dedicate this book to my husband – who has stuck by me and encouraged me with my crazy ambitions from the moment we first met. Without him, by my side, I may never have had the courage to push myself to the limits that I do, and for that, I will always be eternally grateful.

Of course, it goes without saying that I need to thank my parents – without their push and encouragement to always try my best no matter what I do, I wouldn't have had the belief to get to where I am today.

I would like to thank Mrs Gregory – my English and Media teacher at secondary school. She was the first teacher that totally inspired me, I was in awe of every one of her lessons and she instilled in me the passion to study both subjects further and was always my pinnacle aspiration – I wanted to be just like her in the classroom.

I would also like to thank those colleagues of mine who have always inspired me as outstanding teachers and leaders. Maddie Hyland, you were my first true mentor and leader, leading the department with grace and dignity and encouraging your team to strive to be the best. Faye Banks – I will never be able to fill your shoes (literally), but you were my lighthouse in all the crazy, keeping me calm and guiding me on how to be a strong leader like you. Jennie Kellett – You gave me the platforms to learn and grow and always supported me, even when playing devil's advocate and pushing me outside of my comfort zone. I wouldn't be where I am today if it wasn't for these fantastic ladies.

It goes without saying that I thank my support network – My close friends who stood by me and didn't laugh when I announced I was going to write a book. For their never wavering support and praise. You guys gave me the confidence to go ahead and do this.

And a big thank you to all the colleagues I have ever worked with. I have been so fortunate to be part of teams that embraced, supported, and led me to be the teacher I am today. While I can't name every single one of you, you all hold a special place in my heart.

CONTENTS

About the Author   viii

1 **Introduction**   1

2 **Differentiated learning objectives and SOLO Taxonomy**   12

3 **Questioning the smart way**   26

4 **Piagetian programmes and metacognition – How children learn**   40

5 **The importance of feedback**   58

6 **Self-efficacy – Developing staff and students**   77

7 **Collective teacher efficacy**   103

Index   122

ABOUT THE AUTHOR

Cat is the daughter of a retired Royal Air Force Officer, so she grew up with traveling in her veins. After spending her primary years in Germany, she later attended Stamford High School Boarding School in Stamford, Lincolnshire, England, before finishing off her education in Reading, Berkshire. Having such a wide experience of education growing up, she has always been fascinated by how different institutions work to prepare students for life beyond school.

In her formative years in secondary school, she had some of the most inspiring English and Media teachers who started her on the path of words.

Having studied English Literature and Journalism at Portsmouth University, Cat then went on to complete her first masters in Heritage and Museum Studies, graduating in 2010. During her experience on her masters course, she realised she had a passion for education.

Upon completion of her masters, Cat worked as a Teaching Assistant in a school in Reading, where she began her journey in education to where she is today. After completing one year in this role, she was ready to take on the challenges of Teacher Training at Portsmouth University, then securing her first teaching post at an Outstanding school in Slough. During this time, she also took on her second masters in Creative Media and Education at University of Bournemouth.

In 2017, Cat and her family decided to take the chance of a lifetime and moved to an international school in Abu Dhabi, where she still teaches and is now the Head of English and Media Studies.

1 Introduction

Tell me about a lesson that was Outstanding ...

We have all had a question like this in our interviews, employers sussing out on our interpretation of what 'Outstanding' is – this elusive concept, which is almost like a myth.

For the first 5 years of my career, I was constantly asking the same question many teachers ask – 'But what exactly does Outstanding look like?' I have had many observations over the years and would get increasingly frustrated as I would often be told I was 'very good with outstanding features' – but what did that actually mean? I could not pinpoint what 'outstanding' looked like. Was it an all singing and dancing, jazz hand sort of lesson (in which case there was no way I was going to be able to do that every lesson), was it the way certain teachers spoke? Was it the structure of the lesson? There were so many factors involved that I always felt I wasn't getting anywhere. I would receive my feedback, being told I needed less teacher talk to get into the outstanding category, so I would work on this, then in my next observation, I was told I needed to work on my pace and so on and so on. It was never a consistent area for improvement. So, how on earth did those awesome teachers manage to tick all the boxes every time? It felt like a catch 22, never really knowing or understanding what it was that I was doing wrong, and what I needed to change to achieve this elusive prize. No wonder so many teachers get stressed out when inspections and observations come around. What was even more annoying was that my results were actually good, so how could I be achieving in line with or exceeding expectations, but only a 'very good with outstanding features' sort of teacher?

As I was edging towards the end of my fifth year in teaching, I was genuinely afraid I had hit the commonly accepted 'performance plateau.' It was a well-documented argument that teachers are unable to improve their effectiveness after their first few years in the classroom (Rice, 2013). Even innovator Bill Gates proclaimed that 'once somebody has taught for three years, their teaching quality does not change thereafter' (2009). It was almost like my time was running out, if I was going to make a change, I had to do it then, which incidentally was when I decided to pack up my family and move to Abu Dhabi to teach in a British International School. While this myth has been debunked now, it was the push I needed to start becoming more reflective of my own teaching practices.

DOI: 10.4324/9781003264453-1

I had already completed a Master's in Creative Media and Education, in which I was tasked with the challenge of conducting my own action research, which was the first time in my career that I actually took a step back and really thought about the impact I was having in the classroom. It is so easy to put your head down and get lost in the day-to-day routines of a teaching job, working tirelessly to get students through the content for their General Certificate of Secondary Education (GCSE) and A-Level exams (despite what some unnamed newspaper says about us!). But by doing this, there seemed to be no time to improve my teaching and learning – there was a constant battle between wanting to be outstanding but being too stressed/busy/focused on getting students through the work in order to achieve their grades. If only someone had told me at the beginning how easy and weightlifting it is to just take a step back and reflect on my own practice. If only I knew how much more effective I could actually be if I took the time to reassess the areas of my teaching and learning that I needed to develop, and how in the long run this would develop my students more. WARNING – It's a big step, and it throws you out of your comfort zone, but it is well worth it!

While there are many teachers that do plateau and struggle to develop further, there is now new evidence that it is not inevitable – teachers can continue to develop throughout their careers, regardless of how long they have been teaching. As Papay and Kraft (2016) have found out, school leaders have reported anecdotally that there are many teachers who were able to 'continue to refine their practice and invest in improvement well into their careers.' If you are willing to continue to learn, then you will continue to grow. When you decide you want to step into the world of education, you must accept that learning never ends. Without staying on top of current practices, you will slowly drown in the sea of change, leaving your teaching outdated and irrelevant. Obviously, this helps if you are part of a supportive school, where your leaders value fostering a productive environment and professional growth, but collective teacher efficacy is one of the best ways of developing yourself as a teacher. Reading books like this, having a Twitter account to share best practices, and listening to podcasts – will all help you grow in your career. I have developed a number of ideas over time through seeing awesome ideas on Twitter and then adapting them to suit my students, then paying the favour forward by sharing my lesson ideas on my blog page: https://chowdharyteachingandlearning.wordpress.com/, which I have been running since 2013.

I was very fortunate as, when I moved to Abu Dhabi, I joined a school that put action research and continuous professional development (CPD) at the forefront. When I began in 2017, I was introduced to John Hattie and his *Visible Learning*. Like many of you, I started the year sitting in a sports hall during that first INSET meeting, but this time something resonated with me. It was the first time I was hearing about effect sizes and impact cycles; I was being told that class sizes didn't really impact results (something I initially, adamantly disagreed with). But for the first time I was hearing about evidence-based information – up to this point INSETs were always just excuses for members of the senior leadership team (SLT) to talk at staff telling them what their 'visions' were for the year and what their expectations were. This time I was intrigued – there was huge amounts of data involved, case studies from around the world, and proof of how specific elements of our teaching can have both positive and negative impacts on our results. It was an eye-opener – it was the beginning of the road that led me towards being an outstanding practitioner. John Hattie's *Visible Learning* is about encouraging staff to focus on effective teaching practice that enables students in a positive and progressive manner. It was at this point that I realised being 'Outstanding' is not just one thing – it is a collective of minor tweaks that are necessary in order to have an impact. Have you ever asked yourself 'What impact am I having in my classroom?' When was the last time you reflected on the effect you are having on your students?

Visible learning

John Hattie has been one of the most influential names in recent education pedagogy, coining the famous phrase 'know thy impact.' Hattie has worked with thousands of schools around the world conducting the largest research into the influences on student achievement. Using meta-analysis, Hattie was able to synthesise a range of different teaching practices and calculate an overall effect size. Taking on a 'one size fits one' approach, Hattie wanted to see how every aspect of a child's life could potentially affect their performance in school. He didn't want his research to be another fad in the education society, another idea brought in as a tick box exercise. Instead, he wanted to focus on evidence-informed research and develop a new way of thinking about teaching and learning. By creating the effect size calculator (Figure 1.1), he could begin to explore what areas within the practice were going to have the biggest impact.

The interesting thing with visible learning is that everything works – everything you do in the classroom has an impact. Any intervention can make a difference to the students and their learning. In order to look at this, Hattie has a 'barometer of influence' (Hattie, 2012) in which he determined how effective each of his meta-analyses was. Ranging from the negative −0.2 to 1.2, Hattie calculated that the hinge-point was 0.40, so anything above this would be in the zone of desired effects. While things in the negative area are likely to reverse the ability to progress, 95% of things that are usually done in the classroom environment all have a positive effect – therefore there isn't anything that teachers are particularly 'doing wrong.' However, with a few tweaks, you can take your teaching from having a positive effect to having an accelerated desired effect. Here are some examples of different positive and

$$\text{Effect size} = \frac{\text{Mean}_{\text{treatment}} - \text{Mean}_{\text{control}}}{\text{Standard deviation}}$$

$$\text{Effect size} = \frac{\text{Mean}_{\text{after treatment}} - \text{Mean}_{\text{before treatment}}}{\text{Standard deviation}}$$

Figure 1.1 Effect size calculation

Table 1.1 Example of effect sizes

Boredom	-0.47	Negative impact
Corporal punishment at home	-0.33	Negative impact
Retention (holding students back)	-0.32	Negative impact
Summer holidays	0.02	Small positive impact
Distance education	0.14	Small positive impact
Reducing class sizes	0.15	Small positive impact
Extra-curricular programmes	0.20	Positive impact
Average teacher effects	0.32	Positive impact
Classroom management	0.35	Positive impact
Clear goal intentions	0.51	Potential to accelerate
Self-regulation strategies	0.52	Potential to accelerate
Feedback	0.66	Potential to accelerate
Setting standards for self-judgement	0.75	Considerable acceleration
Cognitive task analysis	1.29	Considerable acceleration
Collective teacher efficacy	1.39	Considerable acceleration

negative effect sizes (Table 1.1) taken from the Visible Learning™ 250+ Influences on Student Achievement (2019) PDF to give you an idea.

When I was first introduced to visible learning, I was fairly surprised at how much or little value some of the things I was doing in my lessons actually were. Throughout this book I will refer to effect sizes, and I will be looking at strategies that help move you from having a small positive impact into potentially accelerating student performance in your class.

The question is, are you ready to make those tweaks and changes to your lessons and pull yourself out of the plateau if you have reached it? It is believed that when teachers become aware of their own personal attitudes towards how students learn best, and open to new research and pedagogy, they are more likely to change their practices for the better (Levin, 2015).

Over the last decade, I have worked with and collected a range of shared ideas and techniques that have helped me develop my teaching practice, and I am in a position now where I feel confident with my lessons. I want to pass on some of my tricks of the trade to you guys – maybe they can help you tweak some of your lessons, or better yet, give you an idea that you can then adapt to suit you and your students. I am not here to tell you 'Do this, this and this' to become outstanding – it is not as simple as that. You don't become outstanding by using a tick list (regardless of how many lesson observation proformas make it seem that way). Outstanding isn't achieved by overnight success – it is achieved through grit, reflection, and evaluation.

When I started to investigate the power of evidence-based practice and action research, I quickly realised that information is constantly changing, even John Hattie's effect sizes need regular updating – they may have even changed by the time this book is published. There will always be contradicting evidence as well, people will disagree with different approaches to teaching and learning just as much as they agree. As Wolfe and Brandt point out, it is imperative that teachers read and evaluate research in order to determine the good from the bad (Wolfe & Brandt, 1998). Research changes, new information often rebuffs the old – so it is so important to stay on top of these changes and be evidence-based driven. Don't be suckered by those myths in education – question them, evaluate them, and change them!

The purpose of this book is to break down some of the things I have learnt over the last few years, based on my action research and evidence-based approach to learning. Often, we do things in lessons without really thinking about how and why we are doing them. Sometimes, just fully understanding the purpose of certain activities allow them to become more effective because it is not being done on a whim, but instead as part of a well-thought-through approach to teaching. I do believe that having an awareness of these approaches will help make you a better, well-rounded teacher, reflecting on your practice and, therefore, making you an outstanding practitioner.

Over the next few chapters I will be referring to the research I have conducted and how I have implemented this knowledge into my classroom practices and hope you will find it useful.

Chapter 2: Differentiated learning objectives and SOLO Taxonomy

Learning objectives (LO) have always seemed so ambiguous in teaching, you can walk into five different classrooms, all with slight variations of what an LO should be. I've seen lesson outcomes, lessons objectives, success criteria, or just simply lesson titles. Each telling the students what they will be doing in a roundabout way, but not necessarily really showing what the 'objective' of their learning is going to be – What are they learning specifically? What is the crucial skill you want your student to take away at the end of the lesson/topic? And how, with a class of 30 students, can you ensure ALL are making progress?

Chapter 2 explores Biggs and Collis' Structure of Observed Learning Outcomes (1982), better known as SOLO Taxonomy. This chapter breaks down the different levels of SOLO from pre-structural, uni-structural, multi-structural, relational, and extended abstract. Each level is differentiated to provide students with the skills needed to succeed and signpost how to improve. Each stage shows the cognitive complexity while also encouraging self-regulation to encourage students to engage with their own learning.

As I mentioned before, when observing lessons, it is surprising how many teachers still struggle with setting LO, often confusing them with outcomes. While most lessons now have an LO written on the board as students are entering the classroom, there are still many teachers who either do not refer to it at all or never return to it. It is surprising that something so important could be considered so low down on teachers' agendas in their lessons. Again, this comes down to the immense pressure teachers are under to get through such heavy content, they don't want to 'waste' any valuable time. This always surprises me when I go into a lesson where teachers are spending five minutes getting students to copy down the LO. It is either not using it at all, or not using it effectively.

LO should be considered non-negotiable in teaching, it should be the start and finish of a student's learning journey – a way for teachers to monitor the impact they have had. Students should know right from the start where they are headed and what they need to do to succeed (Wiliam & Leahy, 2015). By using SOLO Taxonomy in conjunction with LO, you will ensure that students can always bring their learning back to that goal and assess whether or not they have achieved it.

This chapter breaks down the language used in SOLO to help clarify to students the different skills needed to achieve. This is why having a tiered LO at the start allows students to find their baseline – they know what they need to do to achieve, but they can also see what comes next. SOLO can then be used throughout the lesson, for tasks and plenaries to help make learning visible and keep students actively aware of how they are achieving the LO.

SOLO can be used well when breaking down different stages of a task, as well as differentiating for the range of abilities in your class. As I show in this chapter, students can pick a task they want to achieve and build themselves up to the harder tasks. Using SOLO allows them to see specifically what the next steps are and how to achieve the next goal. This helps to create a growth mindset because they can see learning is continuously building, step after step.

SOLO can then also be included into their reflection time. Where on SOLO were they at the start? Where are they now? What do they need to do next?

With a range of scenarios and examples, I hope you are able to take away some ideas to help inform your own teaching and encourage you to use these techniques in your classroom.

Chapter 3: Questioning the smart way

This chapter focuses on the importance of asking questions, but not just any questions – the right questions. John Hattie gave the practice of questioning an effect size of 0.48, however, it's a fairly average effect size, meaning on their own they are not necessarily going to significantly improve students' learning. But, if you want to develop questioning so that they are more impactful, then you should be encouraging students to use self-questioning techniques (0.59) and classroom dialogue (0.82).

With effective questioning being used right back in the ancient Greek days, with Socrates' Socratic Questioning, it has always been acknowledged that by using this approach you can develop your students beyond merely showing what they know and understand, to actually being able to think critically and encourage reflection. On the surface level I think we all question as a form of clarification, but what we really want to do more of is challenge assumptions, question implications and consequences, and start evaluating evidence. This chapter will provide examples of how you can hold Socratic Seminars with your classes to help encourage these deeper forms of questioning.

There are many different styles of questioning, and each will have an impact on student learning, but the trick is to know what type of questions to ask, and when. Closed questions are a useful tool for rapid-fire, finding out when your students know on a surface level, but they also shut down discussion. As Martin Renton points out, 'What really matters in questioning is what you do after you have that answer. It is your response to the answer that will close a dialogue down or open up a process of learning' (2020, p. 1). What we want to build is a student's ability to internally question their learning. Questioning the processes teaches students to review their answers and understand how they came to those conclusions. It also allows them to re-evaluate their process when they get the answers wrong.

If you want to build outstanding questioning into your lessons, then you want to start thinking about this before the lesson has begun. While some teachers are skilled enough to think on the spot and develop dialogue out of students mid-lesson, this takes practice. To begin with, you want to think about the following:

- Know your intent – What is the purpose of your question? Are you merely just checking your students' understanding? Or can you use this as an opportunity to break down the thought process? Challenge students to reflect on why they think the way they do. Encourage mistakes and rectify them together through questioning. Questions can have a range of purposes, so it is important that you are clear on what exactly you are expecting. Your questions could be broken down into knowledge, understanding, skills-based, attitudes, and high expectations. The more we model these types of questions, the more students are likely to internalise them.
- Plan your responses – Like a game of chess, knowing and having a question sequence is so important, to ensure you are thinking through how you are going to challenge your students and encourage a tailored discussion.
- Stay silent (and listen) – You want to give your students the opportunity to allow thoughts to grow. Asking a question and expecting a response straight away is unrealistic. You need to allow them time to get those clogs ticking, and while some students are naturally faster than others, you want to make sure they have taken the time to think through the process – if you jump in too quickly then you interrupt this process.

This chapter will break these techniques down to show you how you can begin to incorporate these into your lessons with examples. It will also provide examples of specific tasks designed to build and improve questioning such as incorporating Socratic questions and debating in order to encourage more critical thinking.

Again, this is not something new, most teachers ask questions in their lessons, but the difference is understanding the science behind asking questions, to ensure you are asking the correct types of questions to have the biggest impact.

Chapter 4: Piagetian programmes and metacognition – How children learn

I always found it interesting that we covered Piaget and Vygotsky during our training, even writing essays on their findings and their importance to learning, yet never did I touch upon these guys again. It seems strange that such importance would be put onto them during the start of our teacher training if they are not relevant to our everyday role as a teacher. But through my research into Hattie, I noticed the use of Piagetian Programmes had one of the biggest effect sizes, reaching an impressive 1.28. This definitely had alarm bells ringing and got me digging out my post graduate certificate in education (PGCE) essays. This chapter will take you down memory lane to remind you of Piaget's learning stages, starting with the sensorimotor stage, through the preoperational age, and the concrete operational finishing with the formal operational stage. Each of these stages show how a child's cognitive ability grows into adulthood. Being a secondary school teacher, I deal mainly with the final stage, the time when students begin to understand hypothetical and abstract concepts, make assumptions and use deductive reasoning.

What this chapter really does is break down how students learn and the importance of making that process visible to them. Metacognition is learning about learning – understanding how learning takes place and what we can do to expand and accelerate this process. Through repetition and recapping, using approaches such as retrieval practice, you can ensure that information is passing through the working memory into the long-term memory – ultimately leading to high success. Looking at Ebbinghaus' 'Forgetting Curve' it is surprising how quickly information is lost among our students, almost as soon as they have left our classroom doors. Finding as many ways of developing memories surrounding our topics can be as simple as modelling verbally, creating mnemonics, and other ways of creating visual and mental patterns.

There are many connections to my previous chapter on SOLO Taxonomy through the different stages of how the brain grows and develops. Learning strategies can be used to develop the cognitive abilities of your students such as cognitive acceleration. Using research from Tomsett's (2021) *Collins et al's Cognitive Apprenticeship in Action*, the chapter will look into the importance of creating environments within the classroom to support cognitive apprenticeships in which you make the thought process visible to your students, modelling how the brain works to relate the subject knowledge to the question or task at hand. Just like normal apprenticeships, the expert teaches followed by the student doing and then reflecting on their progress.

This chapter will provide a range of examples of how these cognitive environments can be created through strategies such as flipped learning, retrieval practice, and modelling, as well as explore the importance of understanding cognitive load theory. Knowing how students' brains work can ensure you are providing them with the tools to effectively grow their brain muscles to include more information in their long-term memory. An outstanding teacher understands that students' brains do not work the same way as adults, and so they provide more opportunities in lessons for students to practice skills and understand how skills work so that they can determine which is better suited for different tasks – brain training.

Chapter 5: The importance of feedback

I wanted to have a chapter on feedback because it is something that we all know we have to do but are we aware of how to best give feedback? As Clarke and Hattie points out, 'feedback given but not heard is of little use' (2018, p. 5). With a potential effect size of 0.73, it is important to understand how to provide students with effective feedback which focuses on the learning, not just on the task itself. As part of an action research project, I once timed myself marking a small class of year 11 books – over 2 hours! This got me questioning the purpose of the feedback I was giving, as I was spending so long providing it – but my students were not spending anywhere near as much time reading and taking it in. I was constantly giving the same feedback over and over again. That is when I started researching how I could change my process, allowing students to take more ownership of their own work and make the necessary improvements needed.

This chapter explores the different types of feedback, breaking it down into task-based, process-based and self-regulatory feedback. I have also included examples of how this looks in my own lessons. What I like about this chapter is that it does tie together a lot of the comments I have made in my previous chapters – and it really does show how teaching and learning all come together to help support students. Feedback can include a range of techniques such as effective questioning, referring back to the LO, and metacognition skills. Likewise, feedback can be presented in multiple ways – not just written, but evidence shows verbal feedback can be just as effective. The purpose of this chapter is to give you some ideas that you can potentially try out with your classes – remember one size fits one, what works for one student might not work for another, so it is about finding the right balance.

Chapter 6: Self-efficacy – Developing staff and students

I find that most of the areas I have discussed in this book so far can be better enhanced when we improve self-efficacy within our students. Self-efficacy defined by Albert Bandura as being an individual's set of beliefs that influence how well they can deal with challenging situations. Give a student a problem to solve, such as being self-regulatory with their feedback, the more able they are going to be if they have a strong belief in their own ability. Not knowing how to process and execute a plan of action often leads to failure, which is why it is important to begin building that skill into students' daily lives to ensure they are equipped with the tools to overcome any challenge they face. This chapter is dedicated to supporting both staff and students in developing those tools of self-efficacy and resilience. We will explore Carol Dweck's growth mindsets and building a culture where it is fine to make mistakes – these should be encouraged and celebrated, because it is through our mistakes that we learn how to overcome them.

Using Bandura's definition, we will explore the four key areas of self-efficacy:

1. **Performance outcomes: Mastering experiences:** We grow through our successes. If we are successful, then we are more likely to do it again. When we have low self-efficacy, we are more likely to give up when we fail at something.
2. **Vicarious experiences: Social role models:** Learning is primarily done through observation and modelling. You are most likely to learn traits and behaviours from those around you, so if you see someone with strong self-efficacy succeeding, you are more than likely going to also believe you can have that same success. When we model behaviours, such as how to overcome failure, we teach others to have more self-compassion and resilience.
3. **Social and verbal persuasion:** Don't underestimate the power of positive reinforcement and praise. Self-efficacy is often influenced through encouragement. Studies have shown that many students have fixed mindsets which lead them to distrust putting in effort as they fear their own failure. However, with the injection of positivity and verbal persuasion, these students can begin to develop a growth mindset and build their self-efficacy, which ultimately improve academic performance over time. However, even praise must be carefully given, it is important to think about what type of praise you are giving – we shouldn't be praising the outcome, but the process students have gone through to get to that outcome.

4 **Emotional and physiological states:** There is strong evidence to show the link between emotions and self-efficacy – low emotional and physiological stages lead to low self-efficacy, which leads to low academic performance. There are many ways of measuring students' well-being, which helps you understand them as a whole child. Using holistic data allows you to identify why there may be dips in their academic performance, working closely with pastoral teams to ensure students are supported both inside and outside of the classroom. Well-being and academic success can also be enhanced through teaching students the importance of having a vision in order to motivate themselves to be successful. Once a vision has been made, they need to be given systems to put into place to ensure they put in the effort needed to achieve those goals. We need to build up that self-efficacy belief that they have the tools they need to succeed. The usage of tools like VESPA is explored in this chapter, showing how you can get your students to be more focused and driven.

Chapter 7: Collective teacher efficacy

While we always talk about the benefits of group work with our students, it is important that we also realise the benefits and impact it can have on teachers as well. Coming together as a collective allows staff to grow as a team, building a voice and sharing best practice. This chapter will explore the tweaks that can be made to teaching and learning on a daily basis that will improve our collective teacher efficacy. Knowing your impact and knowing the impact you can have as a collective is really important. This chapter will look into how you can build more opportunities for collective efficacy within your teams – whether that is high impact planning, impact cycles, communities of practice, or a collective language for learning.

We are moving into a new generation of teaching and learning – Generation Alpha. When thinking about how we are preparing our students for the future, we need to start thinking about what that future is going to look like for this generation. They are children born into the digital era, and COVID-19 has just exasperated this more. Mark McCrindle and Fell (2020) have done a lot of research into Generation Alpha and urge us as professionals to start thinking about how we are preparing these students for a future that doesn't exist yet. As they state, 'Alpha – not a return to the old, but the start of something new' (2020, p. 5). These children were born the same year that the first iPad was released, meaning their childhood has been very technologically heavy leading to app-based play, improved digital literacy, and shorter attention spans. I know myself that my children spend probably far too much time on their tablets, even if I am getting them to play educational games. But my 6-year-old is such a whizz at games like Minecraft – already using a language that I do not speak.

This book is about being reflective of your teaching practices, looking at what you have 'always done' and evaluating if that is still working. Thinking about the change in cohorts of students, change in society and technology, change in the definitions of education, and finding a better and more effective way to ensure you are preparing your students for life. I hope that, as you read through these chapters you are able to do one of three things:

- **Confirm** the knowledge you already had and validate what you are currently doing. Feel confident that you are doing a good job.

- **Learn** new ideas of how you could make small tweaks in your own classrooms with your students.
- **Share** the knowledge, research more and keep up to date with new pedagogy.

Being outstanding isn't about being the best – it is about being reflective, improving, and reassessing. Know your impact!

References

Biggs, J. B., & Collis, K. F. (1982). *Evaluating the quality of learning: The SOLO taxonomy*. New York: Academic Press.

Clarke, S., & Hattie, J. (2018). *Visible Learning: Feedback*. London: Routledge, Taylor & Francis Group.

Gates, B. (2009, February). Mosquitos, malaria, and education [Video]. TED Conferences. www.ted.com/talks/bill_gates_unplugged/transcript

Hattie, J. (2012). *Visible learning for teachers: Maximizing impact on learning*. London: Routledge, Taylor & Francis Group.

Levin, B. B. (2015). The development of teachers' beliefs and practices. In H. Fives, & M. Gregoire Gill (Eds.), *International handbook of research on teachers' beliefs* (pp. 48–65). New York: Routledge.

McCrindle, M., & Fell, A. (2020). *Understanding generation alpha*. https://generationalpha.com/wp-content/uploads/2020/02/Understanding-Generation-Alpha-McCrindle.pdf

Papay, J. P., & Kraft, M. A. (2016). The myth of the performance plateau. *Educational Leadership*, 73(8), 36–42.

Renton, M. (2020). *Challenging learning through questioning: Facilitating the process of effective learning (Corwin Teaching Essentials)*. Thousand Oaks, CA: Sage Publications.

Rice, J. K. (2013). Learning from experience? Evidence on the impact and distribution of teacher experience and the implications for teacher policy. *Education Finance and Policy*, 8(3), 332–348.

Tomsett, J. (2021). *Collins et al's cognitive apprenticeship in action: In action series*. Woodbridge, UK: John Catt Educational Ltd.

Visible Learning™ 250+ Influences on Student Achievement. (2019). https://visible-learning.org/wp-content/uploads/2022/01/250-Influences.pdf

Wiliam, D. & Leahy, S. (2015). *Embedding formative assessment: Practical techniques for K-12 classrooms*. West Palm Beach, FL: Learning Sciences International.

Wolfe, P., & Brandt, R. (1998, November 1). *What do we know from brain research?* ASDC. https://www.ascd.org/el/articles/what-do-we-know-from-brain-research

2 Differentiated learning objectives and SOLO Taxonomy

About four years ago we had a spreadsheet sent around from our SLT to fill in, in preparation for a CPD session. On this spreadsheet, there were four strange symbols and we had to put our names in a column underneath one of them. Me being new to the school, scanned the form and saw a few names I recognised from my department under a column named 'Extended Abstract,' so what did I do? I wrote my name there too (classic case of following the crowd!). I didn't think anything more about it after that until the afternoon of the CPD when we were assigned a table and a group, me bumbling along to it, not thinking anything other than 'they probably just want to mix up the departments.' Then, halfway through the session I heard 'can all our Extended Abstract Experts please stand up.' I looked around and noticed one person from every table had stood up, I looked at each of my team members one by one, waiting for the expert to make themselves known, and then I started getting that sinking feeling in the pit of my stomach. 'Come on, we should have one on every table,' our Assistant Principal says, staring right at me. I don't budge – wishing the ground would swallow me whole. After a couple of seconds to no avail, she quickly moved on with the rest of the CPD as I stubbornly stayed seated, trying everything I could not to make eye contact – I then admitted to my table my mistake and we all laughed it off – 'typical Cat.' Who would have thought that four years later, I would be leading the CPD and writing a book advocating for these 'strange symbols' and encouraging everyone to try them out.

What is SOLO taxonomy

So what was that CPD referring to? None other than Biggs and Collis' Structure of Observed Learning Outcomes (1982), better known as SOLO Taxonomy. Now if you have never heard of SOLO before, you probably at least recognise the word taxonomy, especially when linked to Blooms – something we all learn when doing our teacher training. Taxonomy is merely the term used for classifying or grouping and has been widely accepted as part of the educational terminology. Named after *Benjamin Bloom* (Bloom, Engelhart, Hill, Furst, & Krathwohl, 1956), the hierarchical model is based on the six cognitive skills used to develop learning (Figure 2.1).

What Bloom's Taxonomy does is show the growing level of cognitive ability – emphasising the growth of complexity as you move up the table. For many years, this has been used to help differentiate learning objectives and tasks for students, and on the surface, it is a

Differentiated learning objectives and SOLO Taxonomy 13

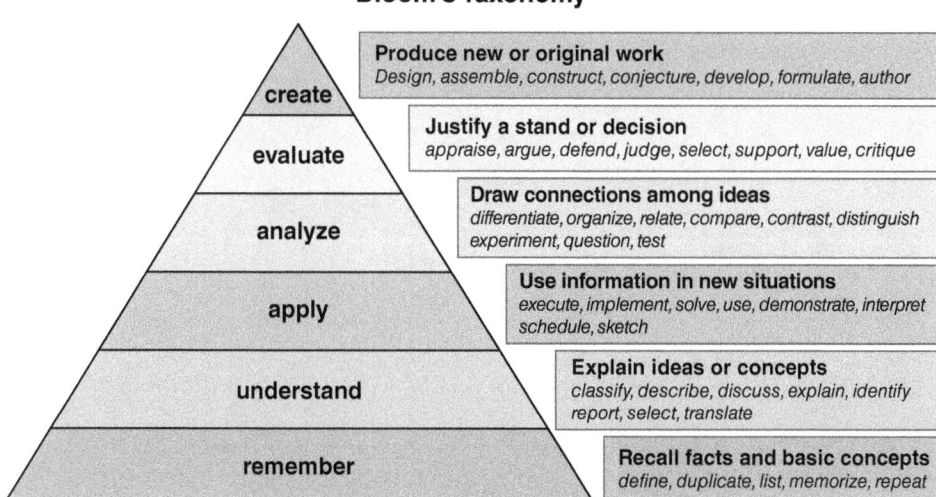

Figure 2.1 Bloom's taxonomy pyramid of higher-order thinking skills

Adapted from: Armstrong (2010). Bloom's Taxonomy. Vanderbilt University Center for Teaching. Retrieved [1 September 2021] from https://cft.vanderbilt.edu/guides-sub-pages/blooms-taxonomy/.

useful tool to understand how to set challenges for your students. I am not going to mock this framework because I do believe it has a strong foundation for teachers to understand differentiation. However, what I think Bloom's Taxonomy fails to do is show the relationship between those skills, nor does it give you an understanding of the response expectations. A student looking at this would not be able to see how learning takes place, nor could they clearly identify the difference between being able to describe and being able to analyse. We can see the relationship moving up as teachers, but it is not very student-friendly or informative. I even bet if you ask teachers from a range of departments and year groups, they will probably have a different view on the definitions of these terms.

SOLO Taxonomy has taken on-board Bloom's hierarchy model but has applied it to structured outcomes. With Bloom, it indicates that 'Understand' is one of the lower cognitive skills on the ladder, however, a student could respond to a lower order question, testing understanding, in a very surface-level way or a very complex and conceptual way. Therefore, placing this skill low implies it has less significance than those above it.

SOLO instead focuses on the relationship between surface-level learning and deep learning. While Bloom's is still embedded and the Bloom verbs are still very useful, SOLO instead shows the expectations of the outcomes. This creates a much clearer pathway for students as they can place themselves onto the SOLO ladder regardless of the 'skill' that is being assessed (Figure 2.2).

As you can see from the model (Table 2.1), it makes clear indications of the expectations at each level, and Bloom's verbs are still relevant as they are still working through those high-order thinking skills. This is much more comprehensive for teachers, regardless of what subject you teach or how you are assessing the students. So let's break it down to what this would look like with some students:

14 Differentiated learning objectives and SOLO Taxonomy

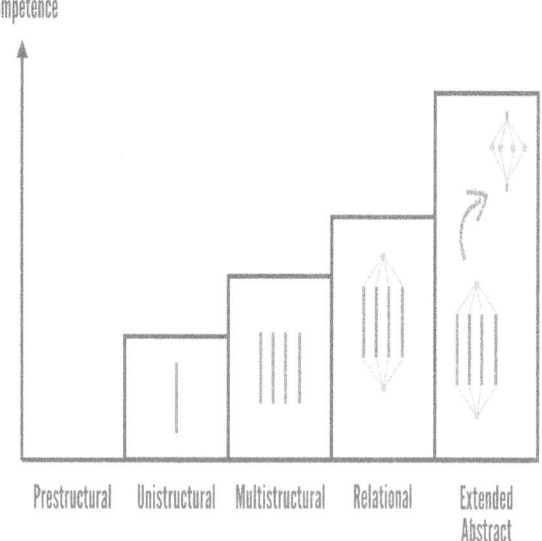

Figure 2.2 Levels of understanding in SOLO

Table 2.1 SOLO Taxonomy explanation

Prestructural	Unistructural	Multistructural	Relational	Extended Abstract
Students' outcomes seem unconnected and unorganised	Students' outcomes have simple connections but lack a clear understanding	Students' outcomes show they have made connections but still miss the overall meaning of the work	Students' show full understanding of the meaning and have made connections	Students' take their knowledge beyond their learning and link it to other concepts
	Define, identify	*Define, describe, list, combine*	*Compare/contrast, explain, sequence, classify, analyse, relate, apply*	*Evaluate, theorise, generalise, predict, create, imagine, hypothesise, reflect*

Prestructual

Scenario 1 - You have just started a new topic that the students have never covered before. It is not an extension from prior learning which they might have at least some knowledge of (subjects like Media Studies, Engineering, Business, etc.) They will be studying new terminology as it is not a subject they have ever taken in their educational journey (Primary through Secondary).

Scenario 2 - You have an EAL student in your class that has limited to no English. They have no understanding of your lesson or how to engage with their peers.

Scenario 3 - You have begun a topic and are reflecting on previous learning. One of your students is struggling to recall information. Their response is unorganised and probably incorrect.

In all these scenarios, the students have limited to no knowledge of the topic at hand, and struggle to organise their thoughts coherently.

Unistructural

Scenario 1 - *You are at the start of a new topic in a subject that is taught throughout a student's time at school (English, Maths, Science). You are assessing students' prior knowledge by asking them questions – a student has a vague memory of being taught it before, but can't expand on what they have recalled.*

Scenario 2 - *You come to the end of a lesson and for your plenary, you test the students' recall – you ask one particular student a question and they can give you a one-word answer, but when you press them further, they are unable to expand.*

Scenario 3 - *You provide an EAL student with a diagram to list the key terms. They can identify some, but they struggle with this task and are not able to connect the ideas when questioned further.*

Learning at this stage is surface-based and lacks any exploration and deeper understanding. You may find that your students start at this level at the beginning of your lesson/topic and therefore, you can begin to develop them further as they learn more. Or, you may conduct a plenary task to check students' understanding, in which case, you know these students that are still unistructural will need a more specific focus next lesson – making differentiation more personalised.

Multistructural

Scenario 1 - *You have been teaching a new topic for a couple of lessons now, using retrieval practice techniques you ask students to mind-map their knowledge so far – the students can list a growing number of ideas.*

Scenario 2 - *You want to test students' understanding, so you ask a student a question about the topic. They can answer the question with some description.*

Scenario 3 - *Your EAL student is beginning to understand more terminology and using them correctly. They can now begin to define keywords.*

Students in this stage are starting to understand and make connections, and they are beginning to dip their toes into the deep end of learning.

Relational

Scenario 1 - *You set a task for a student and they instantly know what they need to do and can independently get on with the task at hand, with little help from you. They can take what they have learnt and apply it to examples.*

Scenario 2 - *You teach the higher end of the secondary school English Literature and you are developing students' analytical skills. Your student has just finished reading a novel and can expand their answers in detail and make connections of themes within the story, comparing and contrasting their effects on the reader.*

Scenario 3 - *Your EAL student can categorise keywords into groups and explain how they link together.*

What I like about SOLO, which you can see in these scenarios, is that it doesn't matter the context of the work – while the EAL student is conducting a fairly simple task, in comparison to the student who is analysing A-Level text, they are both achieving relational status in their context. Of course, the EAL student isn't at the same level as the A-Level student, but in relation to his own personalized learning, he has achieved the desired outcomes at that level, therefore putting him also at the relational part of his learning.

Extended abstract

Scenario 1 - *You are teaching a topic and a student puts their hand up and relates the concept to a real-life example, showing they can contextualise on a deeper level.*
Scenario 2 - *You ask a student to proofread and mark their work. They reflect on it and evaluate its strengths and areas for improvement, motivating them to then go and make the required changes to be better.*
Scenario 3 - *Your EAL student has been able to read an extract from a book, and when asked, they can predict what they think might happen next based on what they have understood so far.*

Extended Abstract is about taking what they have learnt and looking at it in a new way, taking a different approach, or evaluating their knowledge. To reach this stage, you will have developed yourself through multistructural and relational, allowing you to secure your knowledge on a contextualised level.

So, as you can see, it is not a hierarchy of specific skills, one being more advanced than perhaps the previous, but instead, a coming together of multiple skills interweaved and constantly developing on a deeper level. As Pam Hook points out:

> With SOLO, in contrast to Bloom's taxonomy, a learning task can sit at one level of cognitive complexity while the learning outcomes can be assessed across five different levels of complexity.
>
> (Hook, 2011, p. 195)

How does this help to learn

What SOLO does is make a 'clear, simple, and robust way of identifying the level of cognitive complexity' for teachers and students (Biggs, 1999, p. 37). It provides the tools to encourage self-regulation and makes learning visible – students know what to do next, and it gives them autonomy over their learning. Our students live in an online world where they are constantly having to unpack information they have come across and participating and engaging in discussions and debates daily – why shouldn't they be just as involved in their learning?

Likewise, SOLO allows teachers to monitor and reflect on their teaching. The key questions for both teachers and the students should be, What am I learning? How is it going? What should I do next? Students learn that outcomes are achieved through effort and motivation to succeed, rather than fixed abilities (McNeill & Hook, 2012).

Another thing I like about SOLO is the fact that it can be used in so many different ways. When you start getting used to how SOLO works, you can begin to build it into every aspect of your teaching:

- Differentiation – Using the different levels of SOLO means you can use it as part of your Lesson Objectives, differentiating the outcomes for your mixed-ability learners in class. Similarly, you can use it to differentiate tasks, allowing students to work at their level, but also encouraging them to challenge themselves to the next level as well. This helps students develop their efficacy as they grow in confidence with their learning ability.
- Success Criteria – linking SOLO to the success criteria can help to motivate learners to move up the ranks, showing what you need to achieve at each stage to develop their learning throughout their educational journey.
- Feedback and Self-Assessment – it works well with conversations with your students about where they are currently at in their learning, and what steps they need to take to move higher, using SOLO to encourage self-regulation and reflection.
- Building a Common Language for Learning – by embedding SOLO into all subjects, the consistent approach allows students to see how skills are developed regardless of the subject. Similarly, if all teachers are referring to the same verbs, they are reinforcing those skills across all subjects.

How it can be used for learning objectives

Over the next couple of pages, I will provide some examples of how SOLO has been used in my school with a particular focus on learning objectives/outcomes, tasks, and plenaries. Let's start with using it as part of the learning objectives.

Learning objectives or intentions are definitely considered non-negotiable in teaching, for both learning and feedback (Sadler, 1989). Students need these so they can understand how their learning is going to be measured and give them a goal to work towards, rather than them guessing what it is they are actually learning. It also provides structure to your lessons, because everyone knows what they are working towards (WT). Have you ever heard a student say 'what's the point in learning this? We're never going to use this in the future' – but it is not the context that is important, it is how they are using the content, what skills they are embedding, and how these skills can be transferred across other subjects. Wiliam and Leahy argue that before we can assess learning and give feedback, we have to be absolutely clear about where the learning is going. There is nothing worse than getting to the end of a unit to complete an assessment and realise that the students are not equipped to succeed. Students should know right from the start where they are headed and what they need to do to succeed (Wiliam & Leahy, 2015). Ever been to London

18 *Differentiated learning objectives and SOLO Taxonomy*

Tube Station knowing you need to get to Baker Street but have no idea what colour tube you need or how to get there? With so many different strands and directions, it would be easy to get lost on the journey.

When creating your learning objectives, think about these three questions as mentioned by John Hattie and Shirley Clarke (2018):

- **What do I want them to learn?**
- **How do I articulate what would be a good way of learning it?**
- **What do I think a range of excellent finished products would look like?**

By knowing the answer to these questions, learning objectives stop being a list of activities, but instead provide students with a clear understanding of how to successfully achieve the tasks at hand. Couple this with the use of SOLO, and you begin to create that differentiated learning journey for students (Figure 2.3).

You may have specific levels in your school that you use with your KS3 students. We changed our levels to coincide with the 9-1 system, so Year 7 has a WT before the start of the ladder at 1>. We would expect Year 7s to be around the 1 or 2 grade by the end of the year, building a strong trajectory up to Level 4 or 5 by the time they start their GCSEs in Year 10. As you can see from this example, the students in this KS3 class have the levels displayed for them, so they know what they need to do to achieve at each point. These are

C/W   Beowulf – Chapter 5   Date

W – To be able to identify some similes & metaphors and to use some elements of P.E.E in my response to Chapter 5.

1 – To identify and explain similes and metaphors and to use P.E.E in my response to Chapter 5.

2 – To analyse similes and metaphors and to effectively use P.E.E.A.L. in my response to Chapter 5.

	STARTER MENU: In groups...
OPTION 1 - W	Produce as many examples of similes as you can. Write them on mini whiteboards.
OPTION 2 - 1	Produce as many examples of metaphors as you can. Write them on mini whiteboards.
OPTION 3 - 2	Circulate the room, looking at the examples of similes and metaphors that are being produced by your peers. Using their understanding of similes and metaphors, produce a class definition for each term and write it on the board at the front with one perfect example for each.

Figure 2.3 SOLO learning objective

then connected to a SOLO symbol with the Bloom verbs embedded into the objectives. At a WT, students would be considered unistructural and can *identify* the language techniques in the text they are reading, and attempt to write a point, evidence, explain paragraph, although in all likelihood they would probably make a simple statement with a quote:

> The writer has used metaphors in the text for example "Her tears were a river flowing down her cheeks."

At this level, they may struggle to explain how or why this example is a metaphor or how it links to the overall text.

At Level 1, students are working on multistructural, so they can explain the quote a little better:

> The writer shows the girl is sad through the use of a metaphor, for example, "Her tears were a river flowing down her cheeks". This shows she is sad because her tears are running fast like she is crying hard.

At Level 2 (relational), students then start building those higher-order thinking skills, using analysis to show a deeper understanding of the text. They now are asked to write a PEEAL (point, evidence, explain, analyse, link) paragraph, which is an extension of Level 1. They will begin to zoom in on specific words and analyse the effect on the reader, and possibly look at alternative interpretations.

> The writer uses a metaphor to introduce the emotions of the young girl in this text, "Her tears were a river flowing down her cheeks". The verb 'tears' is often associated with sadness as we tend to cry when we are upset, however, it can also be linked to happiness, therefore it is unclear at the moment what the girl's emotion is. The adjective 'flowing' implies she is crying quite heavily which makes us imagine a strong river, so I think the girl is more likely upset than happy.

With a clear indication of what students need to do, with the links to SOLO, there is a path laid out for learning. Students are encouraged to work at their level (allowing autonomy in students picking their focus) but it also allows the opportunity for motivated learners to attempt the next step.

Here is another example of how SOLO is used to showcase the learning outcomes and expectations to the students.

Here, I have used SOLO as part of the learning outcome – while in this lesson we are focusing on 'understand how the images are used to create a meaning' in our Media Studies lesson, my expectation of students is differentiated by SOLO (Figure 2.4). Using the Bloom verbs, my unistructural students should be able to *identify* the key technical and symbolic codes, so I would expect them to be able to look at an image and annotate things like a prop, costume, high key/low key lighting, and facial expressions. To move to the next level, I would expect students to then be able to *describe* what we learn from these different codes. Leading to my relational students who can then analyse in depth how meaning is created, but also think about alternative interpretations of a media text. It is nice and clear for students to see what steps they need to do and how to progress should they be motivated learners and want to challenge themselves. For my relational students, I would get them to begin evaluating their

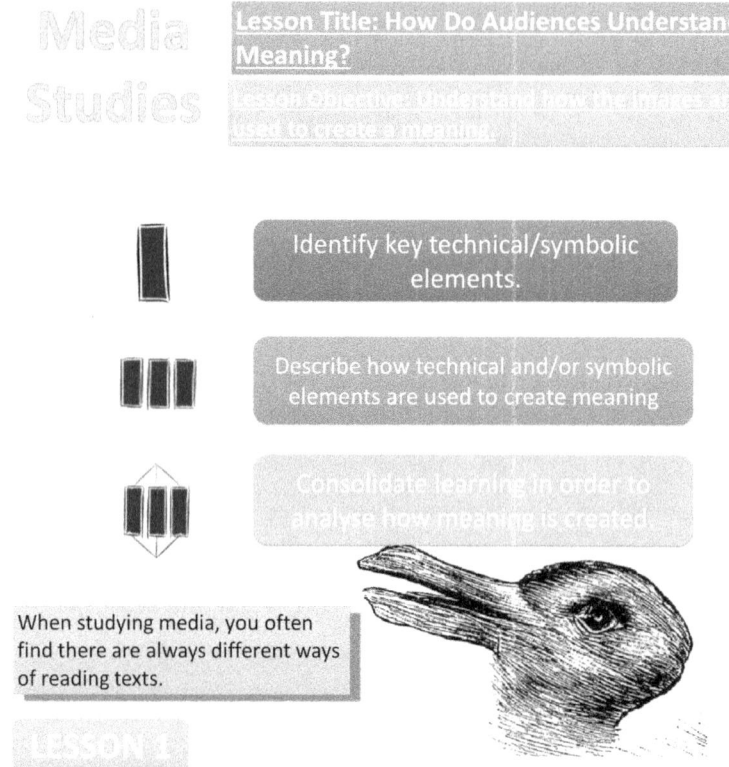

Figure 2.4 SOLO lesson objectives

work and making improvements throughout the lesson. So for one learning objective, I can now assess my students across three differentiated levels, all achieving the objective but at varying complexities. These symbols and outcomes then appear on every slide in the lesson so that students can continue to refer to the steps.

The use of SOLO for learning objectives helps to focus on the skill that is being taught, rather than just what will take place in the lesson. I then make sure the objectives are clear and able to be seen on every one of my PowerPoint slides – I do not see the point in getting students to copy down the lesson objectives in their books, some are faster at writing than others, and this becomes time wasted in lessons. Instead, I consistently refer back to the objectives for students to re-evaluate where they are on their journey – have they achieved the outcome yet? What more do they need to do? Can they begin challenging themselves and attempt higher objectives?

You will notice as well, that you do not have to complete all five levels of SOLO in one lesson. In this particular lesson, I don't have any pre-structural objectives because they have been learning this topic for a few weeks now. I also don't have extended abstract at the moment for this lesson, because we are still building up the skill to achieve that outcome. As their knowledge and confidence grow, we begin to deepen the levels of learning, again leading back to my point earlier – they can show their understanding, but at multiple levels, reinforcing that the skill to 'understand' shouldn't be considered a low cognitive skill.

Differentiated learning objectives and SOLO Taxonomy 21

How it can be used in tasks

SOLO stands for Structure of Observed Learning Outcomes, which shows that it can be used not only for learning objectives but for setting tasks as well. SOLO can and should be used throughout your lesson so that students consistently hear that language for learning. As mentioned earlier, it is an excellent way of differentiating tasks in class and can be used to support students through the levels of learning (Figure 2.5).

I also find using SOLO with revision is also a great opportunity to build differentiation and develop those skills with students (Figure 2.6).

Here is an example from an A-level class, in which I bought plain Jenga blocks and got students to write different types of questions based on the SOLO criteria, these were also colour coordinated so that it was clear to see what type of question was being asked. I differentiated it a little further by asking some of my weaker students to concentrate on coming up with unistructural and multistructural questions and challenging my more able students with the relational and extended abstract questions. Once all the questions were completed, we began our game. Whenever they successfully pulled out a block, they had to answer the question on it. The extended abstract questions turned into homework essays they had to complete (Figure 2.7).

I have also seen examples of dice games using SOLO mats, which again make revision fun, and engaging while also challenging students to develop their understanding. They can work their way through from surface level to deep learning.

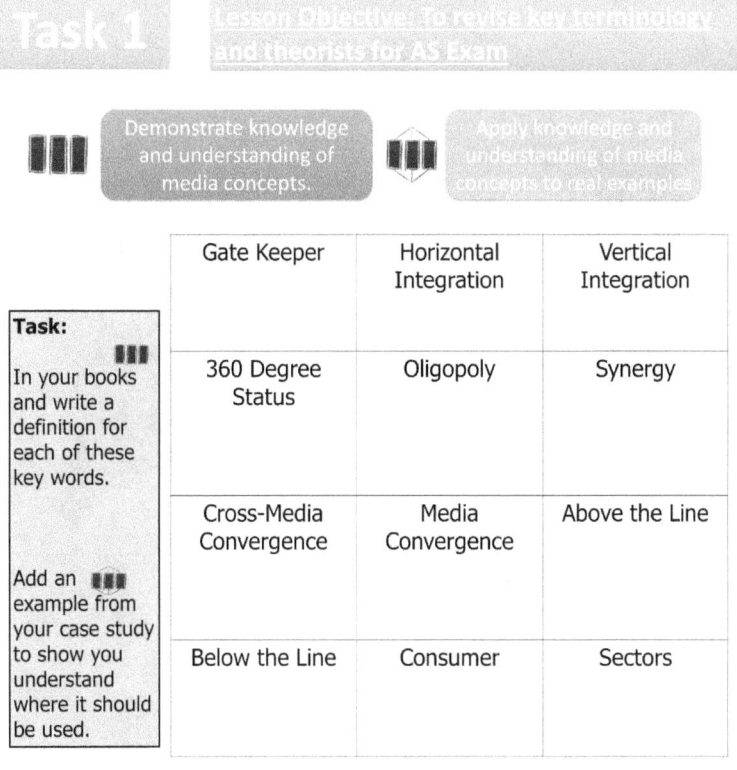

Figure 2.5 SOLO lesson task

Solo Taxonomy Revision Jenga

Uni-structural	These types of questions should only need ONE answer. They are designed to be short, flash questions. I.E: *How big was Disney's budget?* *Name a representation theory*
Multi-Structural	These types of questions should require a list or or longer answer. I.E: *List 5 of Disney's subsidiaries?* *Describe what hegemony is*
Relational	These types of questions should require you to relate an idea to a bigger concept. I.E: *How is horizontal integration beneficial for Disney?* *Compare how gender representation is usually shown in T.V.*
Extended Abstract	These types of questions should require you to evaluate the strengths and weaknesses of a bigger concept. I.E: *How does media ownership affect both conglomerates and independents?* *Evaluate the effect of the male gaze.*

Figure 2.6 SOLO revision activity

Figure 2.7 SOLO Jenga

Differentiated learning objectives and SOLO Taxonomy 23

How it can be used in plenaries

Plenaries are often undervalued, I have seen many lessons where they are just randomly plonked on the end as a way of 'ticking a box' – with little substance to them. But a plenary has so many valuable attributes when used effectively. Like most things in teaching and learning, it is not what you do but how you do it that matters. If you take the definition of a 'plenary' you are looking at some type of completion – in our case, it would make sense that a plenary takes place at the completion of learning – but in a world where learning never ends, where should a plenary take place? And how can you effectively use a plenary to monitor the consolidation of learning, especially when learning is on a continuous cycle? SOLO Taxonomy helps with using plenaries effectively – and they don't have to be left to the end of a lesson, they can be used whenever you want to stop, review and reflect on learning.

Here is an example from a geography lesson, where the teacher uses SOLO Taxonomy to reflect on learning, calling it a 'SOLO journey' (Figure 2.8). This is a great example of getting

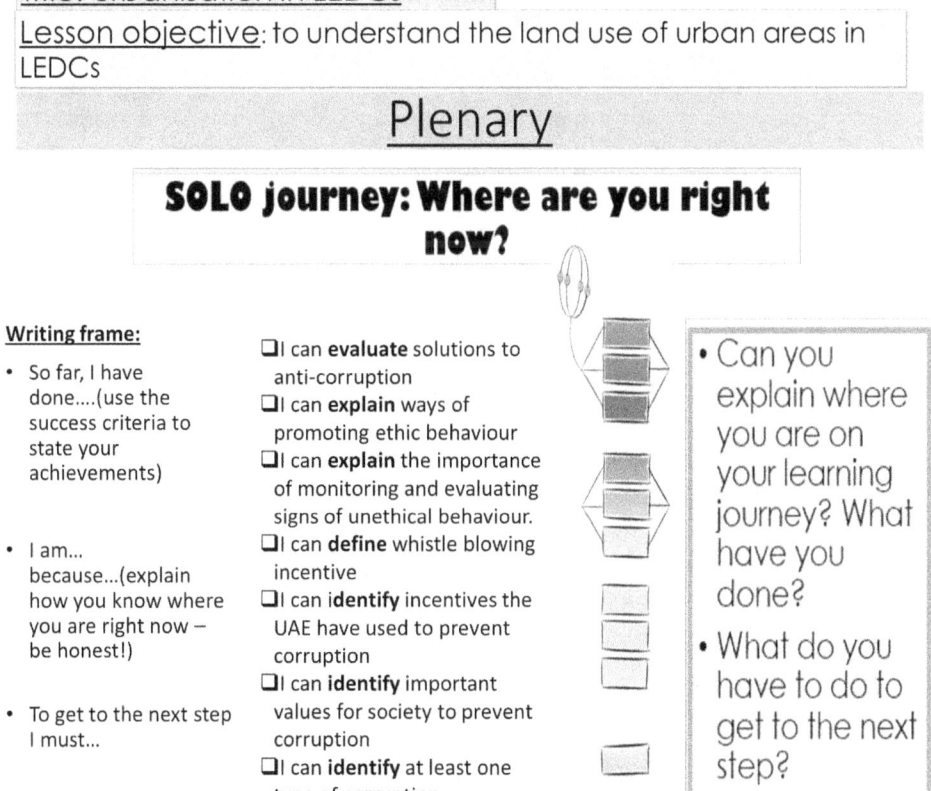

Figure 2.8 SOLO journey

24 Differentiated learning objectives and SOLO Taxonomy

students to see that it is a process and one that takes time to build up the skills needed to succeed in this topic. Having regular communication with students, allowing them time to reflect on their journey – where they are now and what the next steps are – makes learning visible and clear.

Similarly, using success criteria that are linked to SOLO, again allows students to monitor and measure their success as they climb through the different stages of their learning (Figure 2.9).

Hopefully, from this chapter, you have gained a clear idea of what SOLO is and how it can be used. From embedding this into our teaching and learning, we have definitely seen an increase in improved outcomes from our students and a heightened sense of understanding of how learning is taking place, which is often the case when introducing SOLO to students.

Success criteria

0 not met , 1 beginning, 2 developing, 3 secured

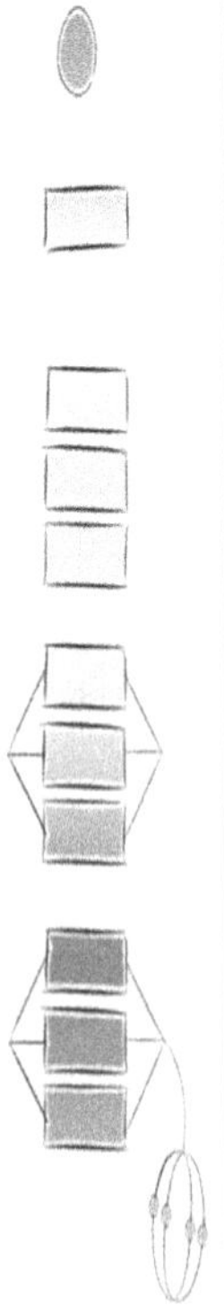

What I need to know	How well do I know it?
I can define the word **urban** I can define the word **shanty town (squatter settlement or favela)**	
I can describe an **urban land use model** for an **LEDC**	
I can describe the **location** of **Rio de Janeiro** in Brazil	
I can describe the **characteristics** of a **shanty town in Rio**	
I can explain **2 causes** of urban **problems** in **Rio de Janeiro** (why favela's/shanty towns exist) I can explain at least one **Social, Economic, Environmental (SEE)** urban **problem** in a **shanty town** in **Rio de Janeiro**	
I can explain **solutions** that have been used to **manage the problems** in a **shanty town** in **Rio de Janeiro**	
I can begin to evaluate the **solutions** to the urban problems in **Rio de Janeiro**	

Figure 2.9 SOLO reflection

> **Chapter Summary**
>
> - SOLO Taxonomy helps signpost to students what they are doing and where they are going next.
> - SOLO can be used in a range of teaching and learning concepts – not just for the lesson objectives.
> - SOLO makes learning very visible and can be tailored towards the differentiated needs within your class.
>
> **So, what does an 'outstanding' teacher do?**
>
> They get their students talking about their learning journey. They ensure their students know exactly where they are at with their learning and what the next steps are to ensure they master the skills needed and make progress in their subject areas.

References

Armstrong, P. (2010). *Bloom's Taxonomy* [Illustration]. Vanderbilt University Center for Teaching. https://cft.vanderbilt.edu/guides-sub-pages/blooms-taxonomy/

Biggs, J. (1999). *Teaching for quality learning at university*. Buckingham: Buckingham Open University Press.

Biggs, J. B., & Collis, K. F. (1982). *Evaluating the quality of learning: The SOLO Taxonomy*. New York: Academic Press.

Bloom, B., Engelhart, M., Hill, W., Furst, E., & Krathwohl, D. (1956). *Taxonomy of educational objectives: The classification of educational goals*. London: Longmans Green and Co.

Hattie, J., & Clarke, S. (2018). *Visible learning: Feedback*. London: Routledge, Taylor & Francis Group.

Hook, P., & Mills, J. (2011). *SOLO Taxonomy: A Guide for Schools Book 1: A Common Language of Learning*. New Zealand: Essential Resources Educational Publishers Ltd.

McNeill, L., & Hook, P. (2012). *SOLO Taxonomy and making meaning book 1*. New Zealand: Essential Resources Educational Publishers Ltd.

Sadler, R. (1989). Formative assessment and the design of instructional systems. *Instructional Science*, 18, 119–144.

Wiliam, D., & Leahy, S. (2015). *Embedding formative assessment: Practical techniques for K-12 classrooms*. West Palm Beach, FL: Learning Sciences International.

3 Questioning the smart way

The power of questioning is not a new concept by any means – we ask questions in order to seek answers, whether that is when we first meet someone, when we are in disbelief about something, or when we need clarification on a matter. Questions are all around us – as a mother of an ever quizzical 6-year old, I am faced with a barrage of questions on a daily basis, usually with my answers being followed with 'but why mummy?' As much as these lines of questions often lead to me not actually knowing the answer to her 'why', I hope she continues to question and challenge answers. As Bernard Haisch famously said – Advances are made by answering questions. Discoveries are made by questioning answers.

Now, we as teachers question on a daily basis – 'What is the capital of Japan?', 'What would happen if I minus a negative number?', 'How many bones are in the human body?' – these would all be expected in a classroom to check for understanding and recall. John Hattie gave questions an effect size of 0.48 which means some impact can be had through them (more so than not asking any questions at all), however, it is a fairly average effect size, which tells us that these types of questions used above don't form part of a well-considered sequence that contribute to effective learning. What helps develop questioning to be more impactful is to encourage student self-questioning techniques (0.59) and classroom dialogue (0.82).

What is effective questioning?

We live in a world where questioning has become much more of a necessity – we are surrounded by fake news and misleading information on a daily basis and should be encouraging our students to be able to question everything they see, hear and read. As a media studies teacher, this is a conversation I often have with my students, but it shouldn't just be in one subject that we encourage this line of thinking – we should be embedding this into our students and children from an early age, encouraging those 'but why' questions. Maybe then the next generation will begin to challenge those long-standing wrongs in the world.

One of the earliest teachers to encourage effective questioning was the ancient Greek philosopher, Socrates, who supported the notion of seeking answers by asking more questions; we now call this the Socratic Questioning approach. This line of questioning

DOI: 10.4324/9781003264453-3

is designed to probe students' thinking and develop their line of reasoning by analysing the answers. By building this line of questioning, you not only distinguish what your students know and understand, but you help foster their ability to think critically and also ask Socratic questions too, using these tools in 'the real world'. With the Socratic method, you begin to delve into the world of asking open-ended questions that encourage reflection (Clark & Egan, 2015). Using this technique, you are able to 'clarify meaning, elicit emotion and consequences, as well as to gradually create insight or explore alternative action' (James, Morse, & Howarth, 2010).

Socratic Questioning doesn't just consist of one or two styles of questioning, there is a range of questions that you could use depending on your context. Here are six of the most well-known styles of Socratic Questioning you could begin to use in your classroom, some of which you may already do without even noticing (Table 3.1):

Table 3.1 Socratic Questioning style

Socratic Questioning Style	Purpose	Examples
Clarifying thinking and understanding	These are probably the most commonly used questions in the classroom, often used to check students have understood a concept.	• Can you clarify what you mean? • What can you tell me about …? • Why do you think that?
Challenging assumptions	This line of questioning is helped by playing devil's advocate - challenging students' line of thought.	• Is this always the case? • How could you prove that? • What would happen if …?
Examining evidence and rationale	Similar to challenging assumptions - you want to encourage students to provide proof to their answers.	• Why do you say that? • How do you know? • Is there a reason to doubt this answer?
Considering alternative interpretations	Encourage students to read around topics and get all facts before forming their arguments. Always get them to question their original answer with alternatives.	• Is there another way to answer this question? • What might the counter-argument be? • Why is your answer stronger than their answer?
Considering implications and consequences	Show students that decisions can sometimes have consequences - question what possible implications a decision might have, allowing them to look at the bigger picture.	• What if you were wrong? • How might this impact …? • How does … impact …? • How would this affect someone? • What are the long-term implications of this?
Meta-questions	This is the process of getting students to question your questions.	• Why do you think I ask that question? • Why is this question important to think about? • What else could we ask?

Table 3.2 Socratic Seminar

Pick a focus	This would usually be a piece of text that can be closely analysed – an extract from a novel, a historical source, a news article, etc. It needs to be long enough to really delve into but short enough for them to focus on in the time given.
Prepare	Students are given time to prepare for the seminar – annotate the text with their ideas and notes. You might want to begin as being the discussion leader to set them off on the seminar, or you might pick a student to be the leader and ask them to generate a few open questions to get started.
Rules	Just like any activity in school, the seminar must have a few house rules: • Do not interrupt. • Questions should be asked if there are any misunderstandings. • Be conscious of how many times you have spoken to ensure there is equality amongst the group. • No judgements or negative comments are to be made if you disagree with a statement. Remember, this is not a debate, but a discussion for questioning the text at hand – you are not proving it one way or the other, but trying to understand how and why it was written.
Create a circle	Have students sit in a circle so that they can see each other and address each other easily. I stay on the outside of the circle so that I become a facilitator and not actively be part of the discussion.
Discussion	You might want to start with short 15-minute sessions, to begin with, while students get used to this style of learning and discussion, but as they become more confident, you might find that you can soon build in longer sessions.
Evaluate and review	This gives time to allow students to review the process behind their discussions. How well did they integrate themselves into the discussion? What would they have done differently? How might they improve for their next discussion? Create a success criteria for your next seminar.

There are a number of ways that you can begin to implement Socratic-style questioning into your lesson. One that I particularly like is the use of Socratic Seminars (Table 3.2). I usually do this with my post-16 students as a way to encourage student-led discussion and critical thinking. This technique does take a little time to set up and prepare for as you want to develop your students' academic vocabulary and model how to have an effective discussion. You want to make sure you have created the right culture and setting so that conversations can flow freely but appropriately.

These activities are a great way to develop critical thinking and get students to ask those key questions about what they are reading. They should be challenging what has been read and how different interpretations are made and understood, as well as reviewing the consequences of having differing opinions.

You may find at the start the students struggle with the types of questions to ask, so you could model this to them or give them a crib sheet showing them some suggestions (Table 3.3).

While I use this technique at the higher end of the school, there is nothing stopping you from adapting this for the younger key stages. If this style of thought-provoking questioning

Table 3.3 Socratic Seminar crib sheet

Questions to see who agrees/disagrees	Does anyone else agree with this?
	Who has a different view?
Questions for when any clarifications are needed	I'm not sure I understand …?
	Tell me more about …?
	Can you repeat your point?
Support questions to help delve deeper into a discussion	Can you give us an example?
	Where did you find this information?
	What is some evidence for …?
Developing cause and effect responses	Why do you think that happened?
	Could this have been done/said a different way?
	Do you think that would happen that way again? Why?
Questions to delve into comparing and contrasting the text	Are there any comparisons that can be made from this text?
	Can you think of why this feels different from …?
	Does this text remind you of anything else?
Thinking about consequences	What are some of the reasons this wouldn't (would) be a good idea?
	Does anyone have a different view on this?
	What are the reasons this would/wouldn't work?
Reflecting on different points of view and perspectives	What do you think she/he/they were feeling …?
	What tone do you think this text is written in? Why?
	Do you have a different interpretation?
	Why might someone read this in a different way?

is introduced and used lower down, it means it will become embedded into students' way of thinking, encouraging them to always question what they see, read, and hear.

Herding and essential questions

One book I recently read that I found really interesting when exploring how to ask better questions was Lee Watanabe-Crockett's *Future-focused learning* (2019). In his book, he discusses the importance of using deep questioning in order to develop exceptional thinking and encourage more questions and more in-depth probing. I tend to use this at the start of new topics, asking wide and abstract questions to promote critical thinking and debate, allowing curiosity to be explored.

- Is there truth in the media?
- Is utopia real?
- Is there such a thing as a 'good' crime?

These questions are all linked, very loosely, to the topic students are about to learn. The question 'Is there such a thing as a "good" crime?' I have used it as the starting point of my *Of Mice and Men* scheme of learning in English. Before the students have read the story or have any concept of the themes within the book, I start with this question to provide my students with the creativity and freedom to explore this topic. (Spoiler Alert) At the end of the novel, George makes the heart-wrenching decision to put Lennie out of his misery and kills him in a peaceful way to save him from the angry mob that is looking for him. But the question I always get my students to consider here is if a crime is done for the right reason, should it still be considered a crime? Who decides if this was done for the right reason? The answers to this early discussion can then be revisited once we have completed the book – was George in the wrong? All my future lawyers like to really delve into these questions, and it is a great opportunity to begin a round of Socratic Seminars.

These herding style questions allow you to then steer the discussion towards your topic, allowing your students to consider your topic in the real world and providing you with insight into their interests so you can tailor your lesson more specifically for them – personalise their learning. There is nothing wrong with exploring ideas beyond the curriculum, in fact, this is more likely to make your students connect more with your topic as they are able to begin to relate to real examples and experiences. None of these questions above has a right or obvious answer, and requires critical thinking and meaningful discussions to develop an answer, they will no doubt be faced with alternative interpretations, 'It is literally neurobiologically impossible to think deeply about things that you don't care about' (Lahey, 2016), so by making it relevant to your students, you will engage them more.

Lee Watanabe-Crockett encourages you to think about questions that will drive curiosity and interest, these could be as follows:

Personal – These questions are designed to entice students into a discussion through their personal interests. You will find these questions will have personal preferences and will spark students' curiosity, especially if it is a topic they care a lot about.
- How can we improve our friendships? (PHSE/Citizenship lessons)
- Should PE be mandatory? (Physical Education lessons)
- Is social media addictive? (Media Studies)

Philosophical – These questions are purposefully abstract and conceptual to explore thinking on a large scale. Obviously, these types of questions can often be quite sensitive, so you would need to know your class well and have an overarching purpose as to why you are asking these questions. I have linked some of these questions below to English Literature as they often fit in with themes from novels.
- What is the meaning of a good life? (Religious Studies)
- Will racism cease to exist? (To Kill a Mockingbird)
- What is the meaning of true love? (Romeo and Juliet)

Ethical – We live in a world where we often have to make hard decisions, and these types of questions are designed to get students to think about the pros and cons of some of these areas. Again, these can be quite sensitive, but they are designed to encourage students to think about cause and effect, linking back to the Socratic Questioning techniques earlier.
- Should cloning be allowed? (Science)
- Is a lie ok if it doesn't hurt someone?
- Can you still be responsible for something even if you were not directly involved? (An Inspector Calls)

Scientific – These questions allow students to explore possibilities – what if?
- Why do we dream?
- What makes us human?
- Are we alone in the universe?

Global – These questions encourage students to begin thinking beyond their day-to-day lives, and think about the difference they can make in the world. Some of the students I have taught had never left the town they lived in, so couldn't even imagine the world beyond. These questions encourage them to think beyond themselves and realise the potential they could have in the future.
- Can small changes have big impacts? (Geography)
- Is a world without poverty possible?
- Should we all be equal?

Asking questions is such an important tool, and when you ask the right questions, you open up a world of curiosity and 'what ifs'. Giving students the opportunity to explore these deeper thinking questions means they begin to see how questions can lead you to new ways of thinking. By using questions to drive curiosity and interest, you begin to see students connecting their learning to context and relevance (Watanabe-Crockett, 2019).

How to ask effective questions

Questions do not need to be organised into a whole focused lesson, such as in the Socratic Seminar, they can be just as impactful in your day-to-day interactions with students. Martin Renton points out in his book *Challenging learning through questioning*, 'What really matters in questioning is what you do after you have that answer. It is your response to the answer that will close a dialogue down or open up a process of learning' (Renton, 2020, p. 1).

Renton also points out that questioning is a process of stepping stones that lead to a better way of thinking – when linked together in a sequence, they provide the opportunity for better understanding.

- Know your intent
- Plan your responses
- Stay silent (and listen)

Think of it as a game of chess, every move you make is designed to get you closer to that end goal – checkmate. Good chess players have already preplanned where and how they are going to execute their moves, predicting what their opponent's response will be and having alternative routes to get them to where they need to be. This is the same with effective questioning, you want to be able to navigate a range of questions to help guide your students as well as facilitate better learning.

Know your intent

Throwing out a question to your class for the sake of asking a question is like playing your go at chess and not thinking about where you are putting your piece, your question will more than likely mean you will receive a meaningless response. When you don't have a purpose in mind, it often falls flat and your sequence doesn't go anywhere, you won't be able to follow up a question with another question, because you don't really know what answer you were really expecting. I know I have been in situations when I have been observed in the past and my feedback was that I had wasted an opportunity to build a discussion with students because I ended up shutting the questions down too early, losing the opportunity to develop extended thinking.

In these situations, what we tend to do is ask IRE-style questions – Initiate, respond, evaluate:

Teacher: Can you give me an example of alliteration?
Student: Big blue ball.
Teacher: Awesome.

Here is an example where a question has been thrown out to the class, and although the answer is correct, an opportunity to develop this more has been wasted. Asking a closed question like this just shuts down dialogue – the question has been evaluated – yes this is the right answer, praise is given but no challenge or discussion has been had. Does this student know how he got this answer? Did the other students in the class know this answer? What was the intent of this question? Where is it going? Is there any engagement in this question? This type of question also encourages fixed mindsets as it reinforces the idea that some have the correct answer and some don't.

Now there is nothing wrong with asking quick-fire questions for knowledge checking, but you wouldn't want to do this too often as there is little substance to them. Where do you go from there? You are not getting them to think about their thought process or how they got to that answer – even if it is correct. Making sure you ask good questions, means you can develop a critical evaluation within your students – 'Skill in the art of questioning lies at the basis of all good teaching' (Betts, 1910, p. 55). Adding a 'how do we know this?' means the next response needs an explanation with extended thinking. Try playing devil's advocate – 'why is this the correct answer and not this?' The first question isn't actually the important question – it is just the sequence starter.

Renton discusses changing the 'evaluate' into 'explore' in order to refocus this line of questioning, allowing you to open up opportunities to develop your students more.

Teacher: Can you give me an example of alliteration?
Student: Big blue ball.
Teacher: How do you know this is alliteration?
Student: Because all three words begin with a B.
Teacher: Does it have to be three words?
Student: No.
Teacher: Do all the words have to be directly next to one another?
Student: No.
Teacher: What word might I have that separates the alliteration?
Student: And?
Teacher: Can you give another example where you use the word 'and'?

Silence
Student: The big, blue and bouncy ball.
Teacher: Good - can anyone else think of other examples of alliteration in a sentence? I will give you 5 minutes to write as many down as you can.

Now students have had the opportunity to go from unistructural to multi-structural in their thought process - what started off as one student giving an answer that could have been an easy guess, they have now been challenged on why they know this, and the whole class has been given the opportunity to actively get involved in your questioning as well with the task you have set them. David Dockterman (2018) discusses the importance of showing students where they have developed mastery in their learning (more on this in my *Self-efficacy* chapter), which can be done through this development of thinking skills, rather than rushing through the 'fastest way to be done with this'.

I really like Renton's five frames of effective questioning, as it really breaks down the process of how questioning can be built:

1 **Knowledge** - this may refer back to your lesson objectives to reinforce progress to the overall goal. The questions are used to gauge the current level of learning. These questions are often used for recall - often referred to as closed questions as there is usually a right or wrong answer. Don't assume because one student can answer, that the whole class can. You don't want to only ask these types of questions - but that doesn't mean they are not useful!

2 **Understanding** - knowledge and understanding are not the same thing, one might know the answer but not understand 'why' it is correct! Linking this back to SOLO, a student can be unistructural by being able to list key terminology, but until they can explain it, then they lack the knowledge of how they are integrated or linked - therefore they are not multi-structural. By asking them how and why, they begin to move into the conceptual aspect of learning. Knowing the answer to a maths problem is 4 could just be a very lucky guess - the question is, how did you get to that number (despite if it is right or not), why is it not 6? Here you are developing thinking to help them secure their knowledge. If they are able to explain where they got their answer from, then they truly know it - it is not a fluke. These dialogues do not need to be all together as a class either, when walking around the classroom challenge individual students with your question sequences.

3 **Skills** - think about your learning objective - what skill is it that you want your students to learn? Content can vary - but skills are transferable regardless of content. 'To be able to explore the history of magazines' on the surface is specific to media content, but what skill am I actually asking of them? To 'explore' suggests they are going to search and inspect information - so what I am really asking them to be able to do is research. Therefore, your questions would and should be related to their understanding of how to research, regardless of what they are searching for. 'What have you found out so far in your search?', 'Why is that particular information useful?', 'Can you find an alternative answer?', 'how do you know that is relevant?'.

4 **Attitudes** - a student's attitude to learning can often be the make or break as to whether or not they are going to be successful in the task they are doing. I talk later on about growth mindsets and fixed mindsets - students with growth mindsets are usually far

more willing to step out of their comfort zone and use their self-efficacy to attempt the challenges in front of them. Questions designed to assess attitude can help support students to become more open-minded. Questioning students' responses to other people's work – either professional pieces but also fellow peers allow and encourage students to listen and learn from one another.

5 **High expectations** – developing questions in this way begins to set a precedent – students start using this modelling of deeper questioning as part of their internal thought pattern. When you use these questioning sequences regularly, students will start to follow these same patterns in their heads – encouraging them to think for themselves. If you just ask one question and then close the dialogue, the students will repeat that same pattern in their heads – once they have answered the question once they will believe that they are finished with that thought and move on to the next – they won't then challenge their own thinking or understand how or why they came to that answer. If you are questioning regularly, students will also begin predicting what questions you might ask and therefore start preparing their answers ahead of time.

Andreas Schleicher, OECD Education and Skills Director, showed in the 2018 PISA results that only 1 in ten students in OECD regions could distinguish between fact and opinion (Schleicher, 2018). With so much of what our students do is online these days, it is so essential that we show them the importance of questioning – question what you read, question why it is there, question who wrote it, question the other side – the more we model this in our classroom, the more likely they will continue to follow these patterns outside in the real world. You don't realise when planning your lessons that the questions you ask might impact the way our students think – but it really does. Regardless of the topic, high expectations of how you want your students to understand their thought processes will stick with them, and transfer across their subjects. 'Effective questioning is more about getting a balance of different types of questions that promote different types of responses from your students, for different reasons, than it is about assuming that one type of question is always better than another' (Renton, 2020, p. 15).

Plan your responses

What are you trying to achieve with your questions? If they are not thought out, they could either end the dialogue too early or have no purpose at all. Start planning out how you think your students might respond – you don't need to write down your questions, you'll probably forget most of them anyway – but thinking through the potential answers and therefore, potential follow-up questions means you are less likely to shut down the sequence too early (Figure 3.1).

In this example, my end goal is to find out whether or not the way Curley's wife is being portrayed in the novel Of Mice and Men (a novella set in 1930s America), is relevant to the overall story. In order to do this, I need the students to understand how she is represented and understand how historical context plays a role in this representation. I start by checking their understanding of why Curley's Wife is not liked on the ranch, followed by giving them the opportunity to provide evidence to support their statements. I challenge them to explain why the evidence is relevant to their point before questioning their opinions as to whether or not this is a fair representation. This would require them to understand the opinions of the men within this historical context. Many would answer this question based on modern beliefs, and therefore

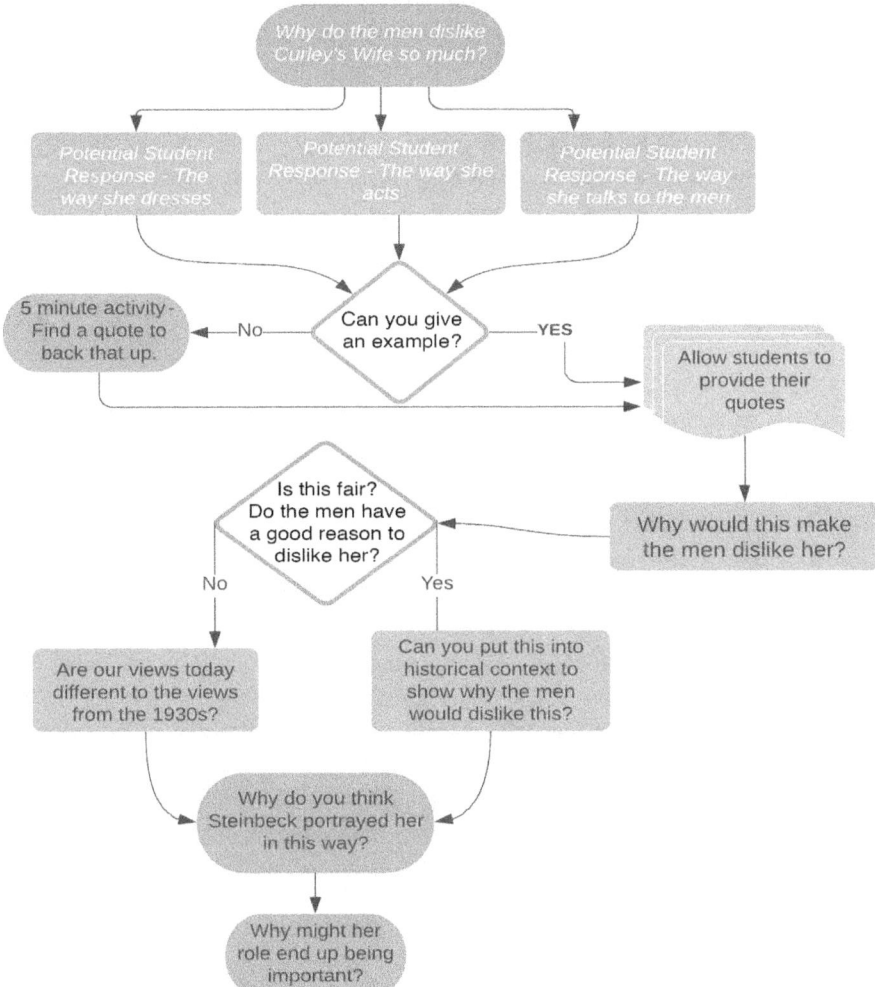

Figure 3.1 Flowgraph of question sequence

instinctively say that this is not a fair representation, however, when put into the correct context, we can understand why she would be deemed as acting inappropriately during that time period. I then challenge the students to think about why Steinbeck portrayed her in this way in order to get students thinking and possibly predicting what her role might be in the rest of the novel. Of course, on the day, my questions might change slightly, or I might be required to ask more questions – but either way, I have planned for possible responses and what my follow-up questions could be in order to get to my end goal.

Stay silent and listen

One of the biggest challenges I had to overcome in the classroom when starting out was teacher talk – I hated silence. I felt that if there was silence and pauses, then I was wasting valuable lesson time, and we all know how much we like to cram in when we are in our PGCE and NQT years. But pauses and silence are good – it allows time for thoughts to grow, if you jump in too quickly, then you interrupt this process. And I promise you, what seems like the never-ending pause with you looking at your class and 30 students staring back at you vacantly, isn't actually that long. The power is in the pause! By building this into your regular routine, students will also see that you expect a response, while it might be awkward the first few times, eventually, you will train your students into talking through and being active in their learning rather than passively listening. This links back to what I was saying about setting high expectations. What would happen if you stayed silent after a student had responded? Would they be searching for another answer? Would they be rethinking the answer they gave? Would they reaffirm their response? Have you ever given them the opportunity to do this? If you can get over that initial dreaded feeling of all eyes on you, challenge yourself and give it a go.

Another key element to effective questioning is to actually listen to the responses your students are giving you. This is a hard skill to master, because you may have a list of questions you've already prepared for your questioning sequence, and an answer that is given might throw you out of sync – a different interpretation that you didn't even think about (it does happen on occasions!). Allow your students the time to respond and reflect on what they have just said. So often, I have seen (and done myself) teachers jump in before the student has finished, they then reword what the student has said into a 'better' answer – that is like spoon-feeding. If their first answer is not quite how you would phrase it, let them finish and then question what they mean, challenge them to answer it in a more succinct way.

Also, by listening to your students' responses and the language they are using, you can get a glimpse into where they are at with their thought process – this can link back to SOLO – is their response unistructural? In which case, can you respond with a question that will help move them into the multi-structural and relational stages?

Tom Sherrington and Oliver Caviglioli have put together some great ideas of how to incorporate more questioning opportunities in their Teaching Walkthrus (2020). Here are some of my favourite ones that I like to use in lessons:

Think, pair, share

Probably one of the earliest techniques I learnt was this one. But this is a really great way of giving students enough time to really think about their answers. You pose a question to them and give them a specific amount of time – one minute, two minutes, etc. Once they have had a chance to process their answer, you then allow them to pair up to discuss the answers. While this might just be with the person next to them, you could utilise this by pairing a weaker student with a higher ability student, so that the weaker student can be supported and guided by the other student. This pair time allows them to check to see if their partner agrees with their decision but also initiates that initial discussion over their answers. During this time, you, as a facilitator, want to be walking around and observing the conversations that are being had, it also means you can help clarify if any misconceptions have been made. Once their allotted time is up, they share it with the rest of the class. This could lead to a class discussion should the answers vary between students. Using a cold calling technique, you can randomly pick students to answer in front of the class – using cold calling regularly means that students tend to be more alert in case their name is picked up. This helps build individual thought while also encouraging collaborative thinking and communication.

Rephrase that

When you have set your high expectations within your class, this should also be seen through the verbal responses you expect when students are answering your questions. You want to support them in making high-quality responses instead of shallow and half-formed answers. To do this, you want to ask your question and allow your student to respond, listening to their answers to validate that they have answered correctly, but give them feedback on how they could have answered it more appropriately. You then give them the opportunity to answer it again, but better this time, taking on board your feedback. This allows them to see how answers should be modelled and gives them the chance to do it again. Eventually, your high expectations for answers will come naturally to students, and you will find they will begin answering your questions to your higher expectations.

Teacher: How does Disney showcase its dominance in the film industry?
Student A: They own lots of things so they can gain more power and make more money.
Teacher: They do own lots of 'things' you are correct – how could you use some of your media terminologies when answering this question? Can anyone think of any keywords that link to this question?
Student B: Horizontal integration?
Teacher: Great, anything else?
Student C: Vertical integration?
Student D: 360-degree status?
Teacher: Brilliant, so let's go back to my original question, but think about using specific terminology – How does Disney showcase its dominance in the film industry?
Pause (allow think time)
Student A: Disney showcases their dominance through their vertical integration buying up its competitors and synergising across different media platforms, forming a 360-degree status. This makes it harder for other institutions to compete with them.
Teacher: Much better, well done.

Here, through support from both the teacher and their peers, the student has been able to rephrase their answer in a more detailed and succinct way. This could then lead to a questioning sequence where the teacher could explore this answer in more detail – why does this make it harder for other institutions to compete with them? What are the issues with this?

No opt out

This approach was suggested by Doug Lemov in his book 'Teach Like a Champ' (2015). When we are not confident with an answer, our defence is often to just say 'I don't know' as a way of hiding our uncertainty, so we don't have to think too hard. When the pressure is on us to produce an answer, we often want to get it over with as quickly as possible. If you are anything like me, you have to internally talk yourself up before speaking out in front of people. Students feel that same fear, the worry that they might be wrong or make a mistake.

By building a culture in your classroom where there is a 'no opt-out' option, you can begin to build confidence in your students, as well as allowing them to normalise errors. If you build that trust that it is ok to make mistakes, then you can begin encouraging your students to have a go, regardless of whether they are correct or not.

Doug Lemov suggests four formats that you can try with your students to help build the 'no opt out' environment:

1 If your student is unsure, you provide the answer and then ask them to repeat it. Allowing them to not have to fear getting the answer wrong.
2 You ask another student the question and receive their answer, then go back to your initial student and ask them again.
3 You rephrase the question or provide a cue to help the student answer the question.
4 Another student in the class provides support or a cue to help the initial student who then answers the question.

By using these different formats in your classroom, you can begin to eradicate the 'I don't know' answers to your questions, and therefore you can build in your sequences to delve into that deeper thinking. While I have discussed in this chapter the need for teachers to not shut down questioning sequences too early, you also want to make sure your students don't shut them down either. By consistently allowing 'I don't know' to be the answer and moving on to a different student, this tells the initial student that they can continue to hide in the background. Begin to build an environment where errors are normalised and students feel safe to make mistakes as this will encourage them more to at least attempt to answer your questions.

Chapter Summary

- Allow opportunities for students to self-question and have a dialogue about their learning.
- Use Socratic questions to encourage critical thinking.
- Ask essential questions to allow students to put their learning into a wider context and the bigger picture.
- Know your intent when asking a question.
- Plan your responses to further questions and explore answers.
- Stay silent and listen.

So, what does an 'outstanding' teacher do?

They think about the style of questions they plan to ask their students to help develop critical thinking. They model responses and encourage students to question everything they read, see, and hear, including each other's responses. They allow opportunities for discussion to take place in their classrooms.

References

Betts, G. H. (1910). *The recitation*. Mount Vernon, IA: The Hawk-eye publishing co.

Clark, G. I., & Egan, S. J. (2015). The Socratic method in cognitive behavioural therapy: A narrative review. *Cognitive Therapy and Research, 39*(6), 863–879.

Dockterman, D. (2018). *Building a culture of self-efficacy by focusing on mastery and identity, every learner (and teacher) can become an active achiever* [Research Story]. https://www.gse.harvard.edu/news/uk/18/09/building-culture-self-efficacy

James, I. A., Morse, R., & Howarth, A. (2010). The science and art of asking questions in cognitive therapy. *Behavioural and Cognitive Psychotherapy, 38*(1), 83–93.

Lahey, J. (2016, May 4). To help students learn, engage the emotions [Blog post]. *The New York Times*. http://well.blogs.nytimes.com/2016/05/04/to-help-students-learn-engage-the-emotions

Lemov, D. (2015). *Teach like a champion 2.0*. Hoboken, NJ: John Wiley & Sons Inc.

Renton, M. (2020). *Challenging learning through questioning: Facilitating the process of effective learning (Corwin Teaching Essentials)*. Thousand Oaks, CA: Corwin (A Sage Company).

Schleicher, A. (2018). *PISA 2018 insights and interpretations*. https://www.oecd.org/pisa/PISA%202018%20Insights%20and%20Interpretations%20FINAL%20PDF.pdf

Sherrington, T., & Caviglioli, O. (2020). *Teaching WalkThrus: Five-step guides for instructional coaching*. Woodbridge, UK: John Catt Educational Ltd.

Watanabe-Crockett, L. (2019). *Future-focused learning: Ten essential shifts of everyday practice*. Bloomington, IN: Solution Tree Press.

4 Piagetian programmes and metacognition – How children learn

Do you remember learning about Piaget and Vygotsky during your PGCE? I think I even still have one of my first essays in which I had to explore their different learning theories. It seemed like one of those things we just did as part of the programme, I never really thought about it again, if I'm honest, not until I started exploring Visible Learning. All of a sudden, these names in my distant memory were recognised and remembered. And so they should be – we didn't learn about them for the sake of learning!

For those of you who have just completed your PGCE and this is still fresh in your memory, bear with me as I give a brief recap overview of Piaget's theory …

Jean Piaget was a Swiss psychologist who focused his research on the early stages of a child's mental growth, more specifically on the role of maturation. This is a child's increasing capacity to understand the world around them. By observing children while they worked on specific exercises, he argued that certain tasks were impossible for a child to complete until they are psychologically mature enough to do so. He believed that children's thinking skills do not develop smoothly, and therefore it is only at pivotal points in their life that it dramatically improves. From personal experience as a mum of a 6 and 3-year-old, I can tell you that the word 'no' to my 6-year-old has a completely different meaning to my 3-year-old – especially when it is in reference to something that is going to get them in trouble. While my 6-year-old slowly retracts her steps and puts down the object, she was about to cause complete destruction with, my 3-year-old will continue to cause havoc with a grin on his face, oblivious to the hell he is about to unleash.

Piaget began his research looking at children between the ages of 0 and 2, which he called the sensorimotor stage. It is during this period a child begins to pick up the knowledge of their sensory skills such as taste, feel, smell, sight, and hearing. These are believed to be instinctive to the child and therefore do not need to be taught. At this level, children are not mature enough to think beyond what is right in front of them. If you have ever been around a 6-month-old exploring food and texture for the first time, you'll know the fun they have with this – usually consists of them concocting a new beauty regime in which they smear yoghurt all over their hands and face. At this stage, they also begin to understand object permanence, in which they learn that objects can still exist when they cannot be seen. For example, games such as peek-a-boo help them to understand that even though they cannot see you, you are still there and will be returning (Piaget's Theory of Cognitive Development).

DOI: 10.4324/9781003264453-4

Following this, children enter the preoperational age of around 2-7 years. During this time, children begin to learn how language works and are able to associate images and words together. However, during this period, a child of this age is still egocentric and unaware of the different viewpoints of others around them. They will tend to be quite selfish at this age (Piaget, 2001). Although their maturity level has increased, they are still unable to expand their thinking skills beyond that which concerns themselves. Enter the terrible twos and the tantrums over every minute issue. It is also during this stage that children begin to develop symbolic play in which they begin to mirror society in their games and assign roles to each other. I will often hear my daughter playing with her friends and the phrase – 'pretend you're the mummy' can be heard. With my daughter being quite bossy, it is usually her that is assigning the roles to her peers, but it is interesting how she engages with her creativity and re-enacts her thoughts through play. It is also during this time that the questions start – and never seem to end. Children during this stage struggle with logic, they understand they have a lot of knowledge, but they are not always aware of what to do with that knowledge or how they connect together.

Piaget's next stage of research is called the concrete operational, which usually takes place between the ages of 7 and 11 years. This is when the child begins to think more logically. It is clear to see how a child's maturity has played a vital role in their learning. As a child grows and becomes more experienced in their life, their knowledge expands. Piaget's cognitive development theory argues that knowledge is being generated through the child's active exploration of the world around them. They begin to lose the egocentrism of their earlier years and start understanding different viewpoints and perspectives. Their logical thinking allows them to problem-solve issues related to concrete objects in front of them; however, they are not quite able to apply this to hypothetical examples just yet. When reading a novel with my Year 7 class, I often try and get them to predict what might happen next, and while some can do this, many struggles to link what they know to a hypothetical future situation. It often needs me to scaffold and support them with their thinking and we decide on possible outcomes for the story.

The final stage of Piaget's theory is the formal operational stage, which is often seen from around age 11 through to adulthood. At this stage, adolescents begin to understand hypothetical and abstract concepts and have the ability to make assumptions and use deductive reasoning. Activities such as sequencing and predicting become easier for this group and they are able to use more metacognition in which they start to understand how thinking takes place, noting their thought processes and applying this to problem-solving. It is during this stage that we should be encouraging relational and extended abstract tasks to help develop this stage further in their education. However, research has shown that not everyone manages to reach this stage, and those that do, do not use it regularly in their lives (Arnett, 2013).

Piaget strongly believed in the development of cognitive structures that provide people with the ability to process their knowledge by making connections with prior learning and personal experiences, finding patterns and relationships and generating abstract ideas and applying them to different aspects. 'When cognitive structures are underdeveloped, learning is difficult, if not impossible. With effective cognitive structures, even

Table 4.1 Comparing Piaget's stages of cognition with SOLO Taxonomy

Sensorimotor	Uni-structural
Preoperational	Multi-structural
Concrete operational	Relational
Formal operational	Extended abstract

reluctant students can activate their own learning' (Garner, 2008). All of which are linked to the ideas of SOLO Taxonomy – building up metacognitive skills to develop students' way of thinking (Table 4.1).

Piaget saw learning as similar to construction, being built one brick and a time. We cannot expect to build the upstairs before the foundations have been built, otherwise, our house would collapse. Similarly, you wouldn't use the same vocabulary and lesson content with A-Level students as you would with a Year 1 student. Knowing the different stages of cognition means that educators can adapt their teaching to accommodate their students through their development in each stage. This will also help to dictate what resources and materials are needed for each classroom, depending on the stage of cognition (Stevens-Fulbrook, 2020). It is also important to note that the stages are not fixed by a child's age – these are merely guidelines, a child can find themselves in more than one stage, and these staged milestones do not always work at a uniformed pace.

So why have I asked you to go back and refresh your memory of Piaget and his cognitive learning theory? Because, as teachers, we need to understand how our students think and how their minds work and grow. How are we supposed to advance their thinking if we don't understand the process their minds go through? Now, I am by no means a scientist, but to put it into simple terms, when a child is learning to speak, we use repetition to embed words and phrases into their brains. Neurons begin to make strong connections when their paths are used frequently. These connections are also developed through experiences and interactions. I once went to a presentation on Metacognition and was presented with this amazing analogy – what is the name of these types of fish? (Figure 4.1).

When you see the two images, you might be more familiar with the first fish than the second because of a very famous movie that specifically references the fish. Even though the second fish, the Copper Butterfly, is just as populated, it is not as commonly acknowledged as the Clown Fish. When we see something we recognise, it triggers our memory. Memory is the residue of thought (Willingham, 2008). The more we see something and make connections, the more we recognise it as something significant.

Hermann Ebbinghaus hypothesised in the 19th century the theory that memory of learned knowledge begins to be lost over time unless it is consciously revisited again. As a result, he created the forgetting curve, in which he shows the time period in which memory can be recalled and the strength of that memory (Figure 4.2). What he found was that memory retention is 100% when it is first learnt, so your students have it fresh in their memory during your lesson; however, this drops significantly after the first few days. So, for example, if you teach on a Monday and then don't see your class again until Wednesday or Thursday, your students' retention has already significantly dropped.

Piagetian programmes and metacognition 43

Figure 4.1 Comparing fish

Ebbinghaus' suggestions for improving memory are to introduce more mnemonic methods into learning to help strengthen memory and use more repetition of active recall so that you are embedding spaced repetition into your lessons. Tom Sherrington (2019) shows in his book 'Rosenshine's Principles in Action' the importance of using spaced learning and making regular daily, weekly, and monthly reviews a regular part of your lessons and suggests the following principles:

- Involve everyone
- Make checking accurate and easy
- Specify the knowledge
- Keep it generative
- Vary the diet
- Make it time-efficient
- Make it workload efficient

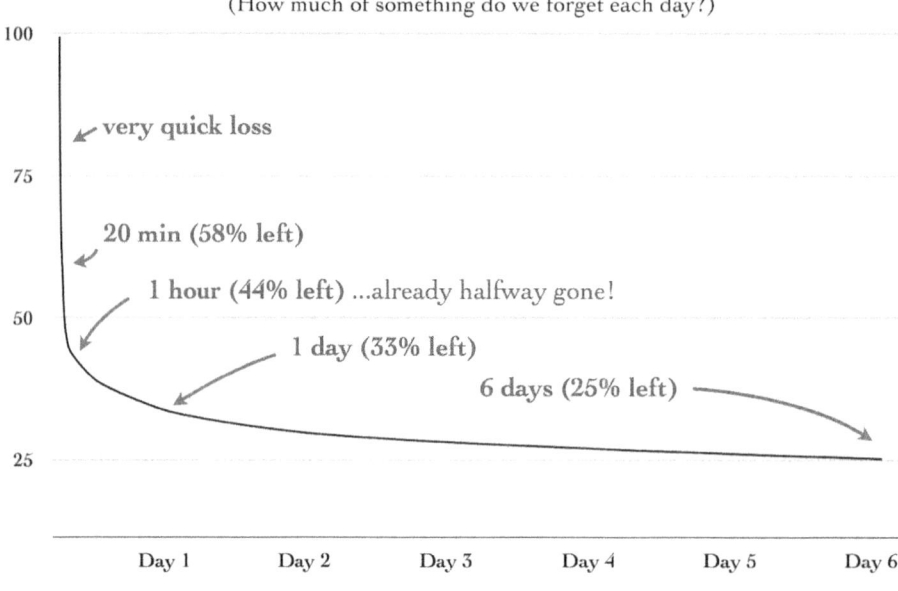

Figure 4.2 Ebbinghaus' forgetting curve

'Ebbinghaus' Forgetting Curve' by Educ320/CC-BY-SA-4.0.

'People usually believe that forgetting happens over time; if you don't use a memory, you lose it,' however the memory isn't always gone, so it important that we find cues back to this memory (Willingham, 2008, p. 18).

What is important is creating an understanding in students of how their own thought process works. The more you think about your own thought processes, the stronger your neuron links become. Who still refers to 'Never Eat Shredded Wheat' when discussing compass points? Or when spelling out the word 'because' – Big Elephants Can Add Up Sums Easily? How funny that even in our 30s/40s, etc., we can still remember these mnemonic devices because they are so embedded into our memory.

Once you understand how children's minds work, the next question is how do we get them to understand their thought processes and become more self-regulating? Metacognition is all about learning how one learns – having a clear knowledge of how one can use skills, strategies, and resources to aid in their own advancements. According to Linda Baker in her chapter 'Metacognitive Strategies' (2020, pp. 253–254), the difference between cognitive and metacognitive strategies is that cognitive enable us to progress in a specific scenario, whereas metacognitive allows us to control our progress. While cognitive strategies allow us to use specific skills needed to carry out a task, metacognitive strategies allow us to plan what skills we need to use, adjust as needed and reflect on the effectiveness of those skills, making revisions were necessary. After making thought processes

Piagetian programmes and metacognition 45

visible to your students, you want to also make them aware of the next steps and how to self-regulate their learning (I will explore this more in the next chapter). Starting this as early as possible will mean as your students move up through their educational journey, they get quicker and better at recognising how to solve problems and adjust their skills to ensure tasks are completed to their best ability, utilising their higher-order thinking skills. Metacognitive growth happens the most in students aged between 12 and 15 (Van der Stel & Veenman, 2014).

A fantastic approach I have seen from a Geography teacher and Head of Secondary, Nigel Davis, was the visible explanation of how to remember how to do 4 figure grid references (Figure 4.3):

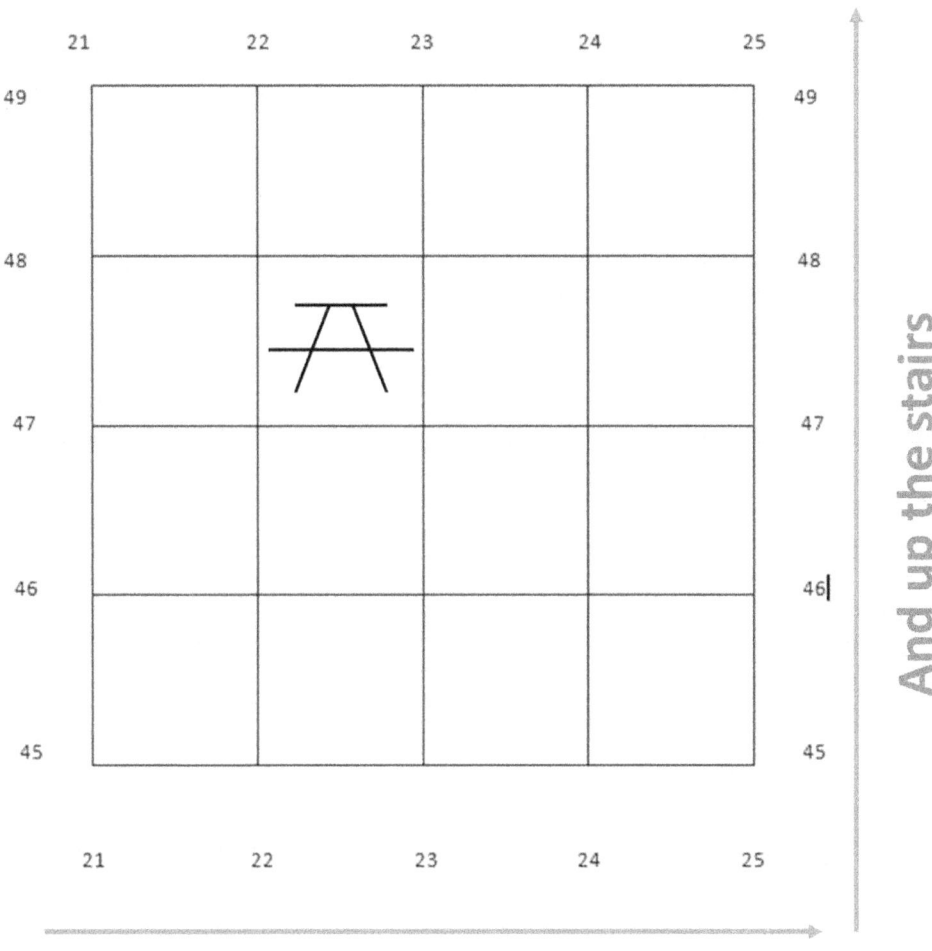

Figure 4.3 Four-figure grid reference

In this lesson, the teacher explains the thought process of starting by going 'along the corridor' and then 'up the stairs' – modelling as he goes. In the above example, when we go 'along the corridor,' we see that the picnic bench is between numbers 22 and 23 – so the teacher then explains that you must always pick the lowest number – 22. We then go 'up the stairs' to our picnic bench, which is between 47 and 48. Using the same logic again, we go with the lowest number – 47. So the answer to this equation is 2247. The teacher then gets one of his strongest and more confident students to come to the front of the class and using that same thought process asked them to verbally talk through another example – expecting them to repeat the same phrasing. Once done, he would then pick a weaker student and ask them to have a go, followed by some noisy whole class examples. By repeating these steps verbally, he is ensuring this becomes habitual to the learner – and just like 'Never Eat Shredded Wheat,' we have created a visible way of embedding information into the long-term memory. In time, this out loud approach encodes the learning and becomes part of their inner thoughts.

One of the biggest effect sizes I have found is the use of Piagetian Programmes, reaching an impressive 1.28 according to Pencil Case (2021). Hattie points out some key case studies behind these types of programmes and the importance to understand that children process information differently from adults, and attention needs to be given to how a child is learning, not just what they are learning. Taking Piaget's initial concept, Shayer (2003) developed the idea of 'cognitive acceleration.' Traditional research focuses on two broad principles: (1) children's intellect develops with age and (2) general intellect is influenced by both environment and maturation. With the introduction of cognitive acceleration, the idea is to stimulate and advance intellect beyond the natural speed of maturation through the use of specially designed thinking lessons. By developing these types of programmes, the intention is to improve students' intellectual capacity and ultimately school achievement (Millar, Venville, & Oliver, 2014). It was through intensive research into the teaching of Science, and later on Maths too, that Shayer was able to present the results of his finding, showcasing that within a class, you could have students with significant differences in their cognitive abilities, meaning while some could work at the abstract formal operational stage, there were a number of students who couldn't. 'If you cannot assess the range of mental levels of the children in your class, and simultaneously what is the level of cognitive demand of each of the lesson activity, how can you plan and then execute … tactics which result in all engaging fruitfully?' (Shayer, 2003, p. 481).

As part of Shayer's programme, there are three main ideas:

- You can develop the mind through increased challenge or disequilibrium, so you must incorporate intervention that provides cognitive conflict.
- The mind develops as we become more conscious of how the mind works and understand the processes that are taking place.
- Cognitive development is further enhanced through high-quality dialogue in social interactions with peers.

As I mentioned earlier, Piaget suggested that the formal operational stage usually started around the age of 11; however, Shayer's research tells us that this has actually been gradually increasing and fewer than 50% of students in Years 11 and 12 in the UK are formal operational thinkers. Shayer puts this down to the fact that these students are tested on the accumulation of knowledge for their GCSEs to the detriment of higher-order thinking skills. What you see happening is the rush to get all content covered by teachers, that these skills are not seen as a key priority. Then we are faced with bigger gaps between GCSE, A-Levels and further education. But nothing is stopping us from developing these skills – even with the time constraints of exam pressure. It is about using the time you have to generate the biggest effect.

Retrieval practice

Retrieval practice is a fantastic learning strategy that supports cognitive development. Instead of leaving revision techniques until the end of a topic or unit, retrieval practice can be embedded throughout the learning in order to move knowledge from the short-term memory into the long-term memory. Karpicke (2012) wrote that 'practicing retrieval does not merely produce rote, transient learning; it produces meaningful, long-term learning.' The old saying 'use it or lose it' couldn't be more true for students' knowledge – you as a classroom teacher know they have been given the information, so why can't they recall it when you set the end of term assessment? Because the period of time has been too long.

Kate Jones (2019) has picked out ten great effects of implementing retrieval practice into your lessons:

1. Aids later retention of knowledge
2. Identifies any gaps in students' knowledge
3. Students can learn more from the next learning period with retrieval practice testing
4. Creates better organisation of knowledge
5. Helps to transfer knowledge to a new context
6. Allows knowledge to be retrieved even if it wasn't in the test
7. Improves metacognitive monitoring
8. Supports the ability to prior learning getting confused with new learning
9. Gives feedback to teachers
10. Encourages more studying

Using some of Kate Jones' ideas from her 'Retrieval Practice: Resources Guide: Ideas & Activities for the Classroom' (2021), I began to make an active decision to start embedding retrieval practice into my lessons on a regular basis to ensure learning moved from the short term to the long term memory so that my students would feel better prepared for assessments, rather than leaving retrieval to the end during their revision stage (Figure 4.4).

In this lesson I got my students to recall their knowledge to help them structure an exam question. Using the hints to guide them, they had to recall the information needed for each step to get them to the finish line. This could then be used as their essay plan when asked to do a timed question.

I used this with my exam classes to help them delve more into their analysis, as I found they were only giving surface information and not really expanding on their answers.

48 Piagetian programmes and metacognition

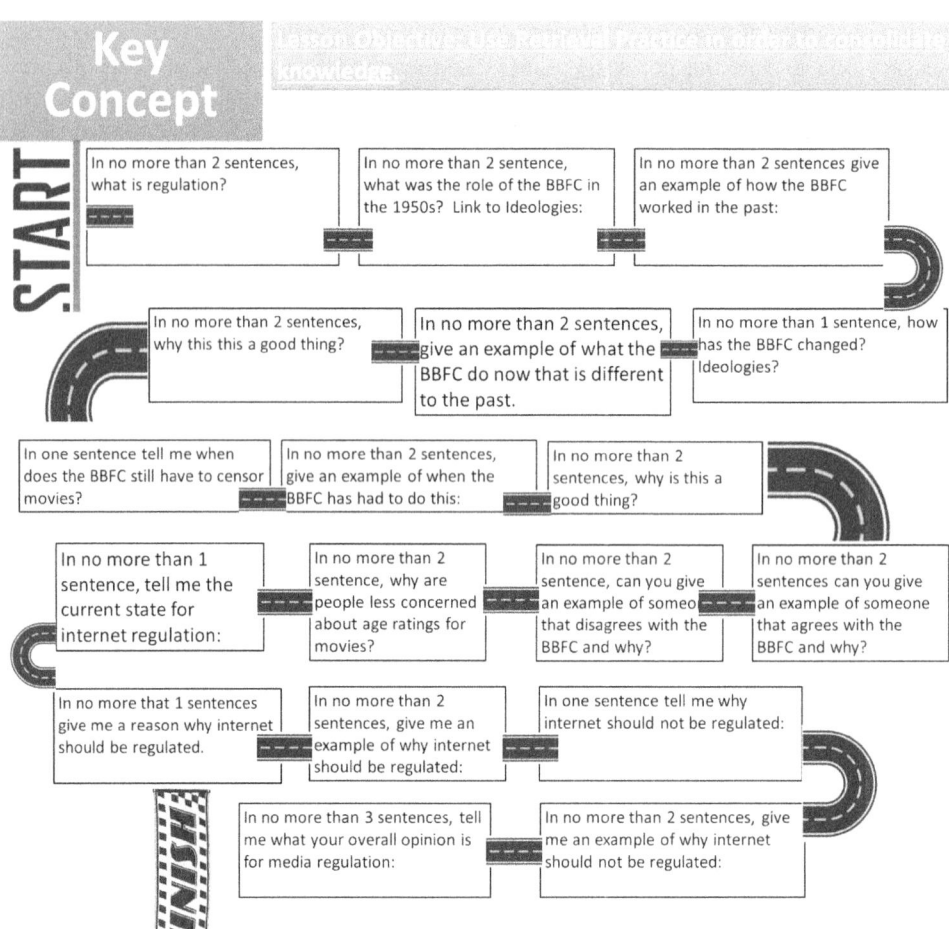

Figure 4.4 Retrieval practice road map

This activity forced them to think deeper about their answer and think about the 'why' aspect of what they were saying (Table 4.2).

Another tool I like to use is Kahoot – I will often create new Kahoot quizzes as part of their retrieval practice to refresh their learning. With my Year 9 class, I repeat the same Kahoot quiz at different stages to keep their knowledge fresh.

Now of course there has been some scepticism regarding Ebbinghaus' forgetting curve, mainly because this research was conducted in 1885 and Ebbinghaus did the experiment on himself. Another critical evaluation of the forgetting curve, as pointed out by Praveen Shrestha (2017), is the impact of other factors on your memory such as significant or shocking events that can be imprinted in your memory. However, there have been more recent replicas of the original experiment, reaching very similar results (Murre & Dros, 2015). John Hattie also agrees with the idea that we need to repeatedly learn skills so that they become automatic, moving to our long-term memory (Clarke & Hattie, 2018).

Table 4.2 Expand and elaborate activity

Statement	Expand (Because/Such as/For Example)	Elaborate
In this scene, the audience is made aware of the tense atmosphere.	For example, the director intentionally uses the symbolic codes of lighting in the mise-en-scene, making the scene dark with shadows.	Relating to Saussure's semiotics, I think that using shadows, we connote that this is a sign of mystery and fear. It makes the audience afraid of what might happen next in the scene, building up suspense and terror. I believe this was the director's preferred reading.

Cognitive apprenticeship

With a mixed ability class of 30 students, who have a wide range of target grades from 9 to 3 at GCSE, coupled with a department target of raising the attainment and percentages of 9–5 grades, pressure can feel very overwhelming at times. Many subjects race through the content to ensure all the knowledge needed for the exams has been covered, but then when they get their students to sit mocks or in class practice assessments, they are surprised by how low they can often score. This is because the 'domain (subject) knowledge … provides insufficient clues for many students about how to actually go about solving problems and carrying out tasks in a domain' (Tomsett, 2021, p. 7), meaning they don't actually know how to take this knowledge and put it into problem-solving context. What *Collins et al* suggest is creating environments within the classroom to support cognitive apprenticeships in which you make the thought process visible to your students, modelling how the brain works to relate the subject knowledge to the question or task at hand. Just like normal apprenticeships, the expert teaches followed by the student doing and then reflecting on their progress. In order to do this, *Collins et al* break this process down into four principles (Table 4.3).

The importance of embedding these practices to develop cognitive ability is explained by the EEF report that 'to move from novice to expert, our pupils need to know how an expert athlete, artist, historian, or scientist habitually thinks and acts. We need to make these largely implicit processes explicit to our novice learners' (Quigley, Muijs, & Stringer, 2018, p. 16). While I have shown some examples of these techniques in previous chapters (and will cover more in the next chapters), I will show some examples of how I implement some of these techniques into my lessons below.

Modelling

I will often use the modelling technique and make my thought process visible to my students when looking at exam questions (Figure 4.5). Often students don't achieve higher marks in an exam because they have not read the question properly, so I think it is important to discuss this with students and show them how to break down the questions.

Table 4.3 Four principles of cognitive apprenticeship

Principles	Key Elements	Explanation	Some Examples
Content – the key knowledge that needs to be learnt	Domain knowledge	Specific facts needed for the topic/subject	• Teacher-directed
	Heuristic strategies	Techniques of how to complete the task	• Research challenges
	Control strategies	Students managing their own learning	• Writing PEE (point, evidence, explain) paragraphs
	Learning strategies	Understanding different ways of learning new content	• Reading
			• Video tutorials
			• Flipped learning
			• Retrieval practice
			• Applying knowledge to examples
			• RAG [Red (dark), Amber (bold), Green (light)] levels of understanding of knowledge
Method – the type of teaching needed to get the information across to students	Modelling	The teacher does the task first	• Flipped learning
	Coaching	The teacher facilitates the learning while students attempt the task	• 'I do/we do/you do'
	Scaffolding	Rubix and support to help students through the steps	• Mark schemes
	Articulation	Discussions to verbalise ideas and answers	• Success criteria
	Reflection	Comparing answers with peers, seeing where improvements could be made	• Close exercises
	Exploration	Opportunities to solve problems and make amendments	• Keyword matching
			• Socratic Questioning
			• Think, pair, share
			• Peer marking
			• WWW/EBI
			• DIRT (Directed Improvement and Reflection Time)
			• Purple Pens
Sequencing – increasing the difficulty as the task grows to ensure a challenge is taking place	Global before local skills	Looking at the bigger picture first	• Connecting to the bigger outcome
	Increasing complexity	Gradually making tasks more difficult for students	• SOLO tasks
	Increasing diversity	Provide more than one scenario so that students can apply their knowledge in different ways	• Wide range of tasks to choose from
			• Socratic Questioning
			• Apply to different examples
Sociology – the environment in which learning can grow	Situated learning	Apply tasks to real-world scenarios	• Make the lesson relevant to their lives
	Community of practice	Working together to find different ways of completing the task	• Group work with roles
	Intrinsic motivation	Creating personal goals for improvement	• Lead learners
	Cooperation	Teamwork amongst peers	• Students becoming teachers
			• Reflection/DIRT
			• Goal setting

Piagetian programmes and metacognition 51

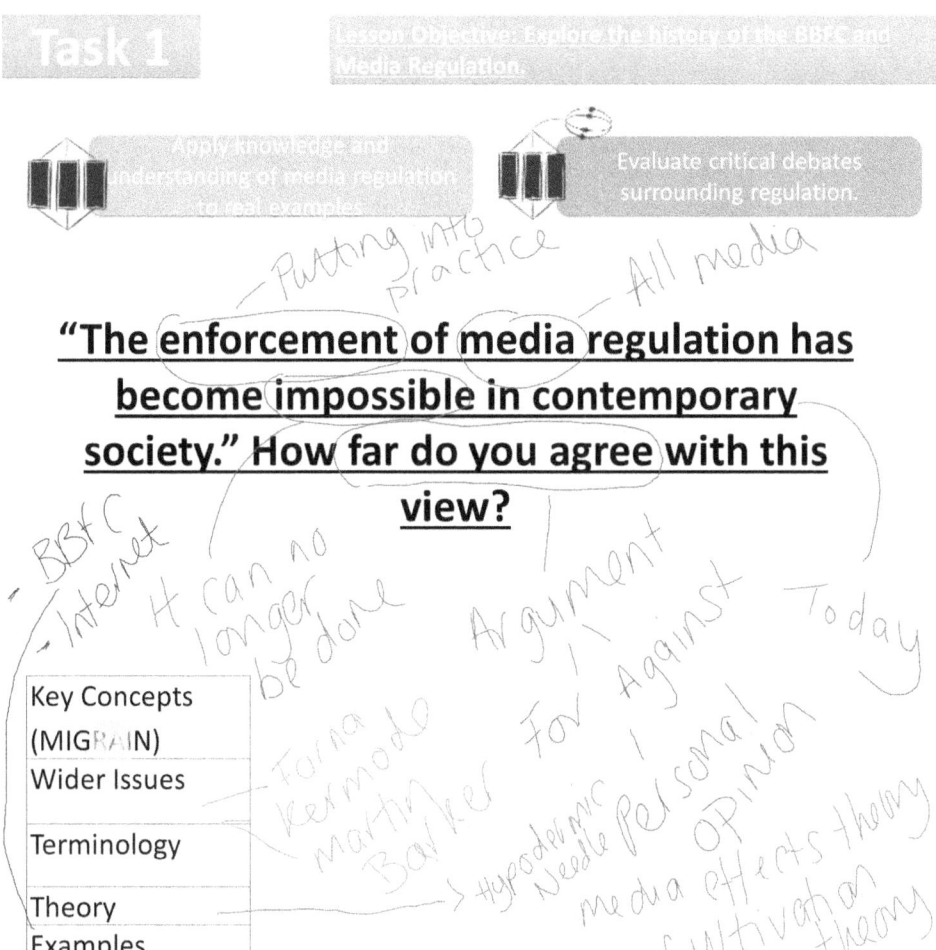

Figure 4.5 Modelling and exam question

By talking through the question with my students, they can see how important it is to zoom into each of the words in the question to make sure they have understood the whole section. Often students will see the phrase 'how far do you agree with this view,' and they will just give a one-sided account and not explore both sides of an argument. I also keep the key sections of the mark scheme on the board as well to remind them of what needs to be covered within the answer. I would then give them a different question and get them to do the same thing, practicing breaking down their own question, followed by then discussing with their peers their understanding of the question and the different approaches to answering it.

Once students have practiced breaking down exam questions, I will also model how to write a paragraph for them (Figure 4.6).

Eventually, you begin to fade out the scaffolding to encourage more independent learning and allow students to take more autonomy of their work. You may have noticed how relevant modelling is in many of my chapters so far, we will come back to modelling again later on too.

52 Piagetian programmes and metacognition

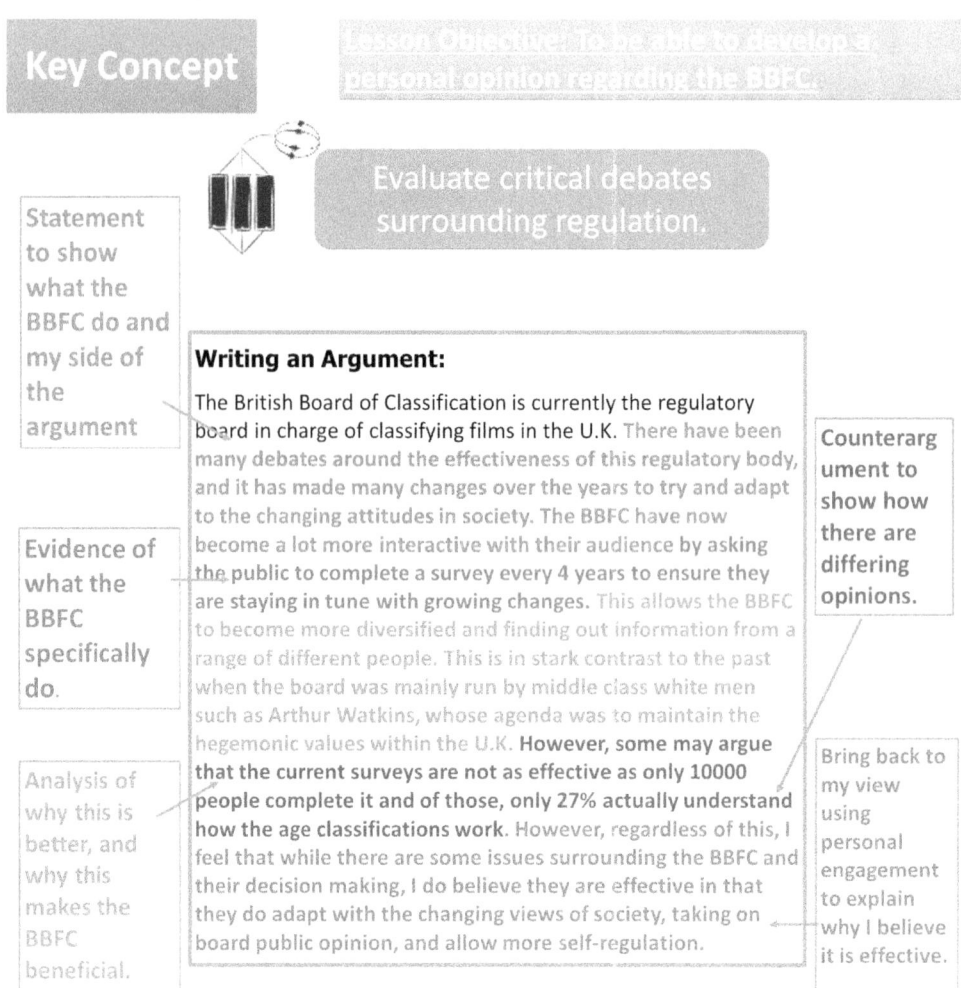

Figure 4.6 Modelling paragraph writing

Group work

To bring in a sense of community practice with my students is through creating four groups each with a different question. Giving them 5 minutes to break down the question, they then rotate round to a new question. Using the notes from the previous group, they are then given 7 minutes to collectively write the first paragraph, followed by rotating again, reading the notes and paragraph 1 from the previous groups they then have 7 minutes to write the next paragraph and so on until they have four paragraphs written for each question.

Questioning and discussion

As I mentioned in my previous chapter, questioning and classroom discussions are a great way to build Piagetian strategies into your lessons. By knowing your intent and planning in your question sequences, you can begin to model and scaffold that thinking process, encouraging your students to incorporate that into their own learning. Building in more complex and abstract questions makes the activity become more constructivist and can help move students into the formal operational stage. Not only this, but by including more classroom discussions, it allows you to be silent and observe the responses of your students – this will teach you a lot about where they are in the cognitive stages and ultimately allow you to understand how they need to be developed. While you should never pigeonhole students into set groups, this initial information will tell you about their starting point and how to move them all forward to progress individually. To begin a discussion or ask a question, you can see whether your student has the capacity to engage with this task or whether you have stretched them past their personal range of development, allowing you to measure stretch and challenge in your lesson. Students often rely heavily on their own experiences, so opening up discussions to the class allows them to see other viewpoints and ideas and so they begin to learn vicariously (more on this to come later in the book).

Flipped learning

When I was starting out as a teacher, one of my biggest criticisms was that there was too much teacher talk. This always confused me because I was always worried that without the teacher talk the content wouldn't get covered. So, what I started to do was implement more flipped learning strategies into my lessons.

Flipped learning has definitely become easier since COVID and distance learning began. It is exactly what it sounds like, literally flipping the traditional classroom so that the knowledge and course content is done at home so that lesson time can be used to explore those higher-order thinking skills. By doing this, the teacher becomes more of a facilitator, facilitating the learning and discussions taking place amongst the students. Pretty much like when we were at university and we had to come to our seminars prepared with that week's reading so that we can discuss our understanding and delve into the content more. Nobody wanted to be that one student that didn't do the work, sitting silently at the back praying that the lecturer didn't ask you a question. By incorporating flipped learning into your lesson, you eliminate the 'one size fits all' didactic style of teaching and instead target support to the students that really need it.

With a flipped learning approach, direct instructions can move away from the group learning space to the individual learning space, putting the individual in control of their own learning and allowing the classroom to become a dynamic, interactive learning environment where the 'facilitator' role is to guide and support the learning taking place. Uni-structural and Multi-structural tasks can be provided online before the lesson so that application and deeper understanding can be met once in class. In a traditional learning environment, students acquired knowledge within the classroom but were sent away to try and synthesise, analyse, and evaluate that knowledge at home, whereas with the flipped approach, students can acquire this knowledge 'prior' to the lesson through the use of pre-recordings by the teacher/videos/reading material/online tutorials, so that limited amount of classroom contact time we have with students can be better used to practice and apply concepts and ideas through interactions with their peers. Tasks are still differentiated in class to encourage stretch and challenge, but they will apply their knowledge from the 'pre-learning' materials to develop a deeper level of understanding.

An online survey of 450 teachers conducted in 2012 by the Flipped Learning Network in conjunction with ClassroomWindow found that teachers associate Flipped Learning with improved student performance and attitudes, and increased job satisfaction. Of the teachers surveyed, 67% reported their students' standardized test scores increased after flipping their classrooms. In the same survey, 80% of teachers perceived an improvement in their students' attitudes towards learning. Nearly nine in ten of the teachers surveyed reported that their job satisfaction also improved, with 46% reporting significant improvement (Classroom Window, n.d.). A substantial body of research on student-centred, active learning strategies supports the effectiveness of these approaches in increasing student learning and achievement. Using a flipped learning active approach has been associated with bettering academic performance (Michael, 2006) and 'increased student engagement, critical thinking, and better attitudes toward learning' (O'Dowd & Aguilar-Roca, 2009). When problem-based active learning occurs in science courses, for example, students report learning more, and their attitudes towards class improve (Akınoğlu & Tandoğan, 2007). Moreover, misconceptions are significantly reduced.

With the growth of technology over the last 2 years, I have really delved into the world of pre-work rather than homework. Instead, I will provide students with either material or even recorded videos of me discussing context, which students can access at home and learn at their own pace. As Lee Watanabe-Crockett points out, 'on-demand flipped learning materials make content available to those who struggle slightly more to absorb learning to review it as much as they need to' (2019, p. 39). Another way I flip learning is by encouraging more literacy with my students. Creating an online Padlet, I upload weekly reading material and get students to make comments on the Padlet about what they have just read. Here is an example of how I implement flipped learning into a typical lesson (Table 4.4).

Cognitive load theory

One thing you want to avoid when learning new content is overstretching the cognitive load of your students. Think of their brains like a word document on the computer. When you are typing long essays and saving your work to the desktop, it is using the working memory – which can often crash, leaving your screen to go all misty and giving you the option to either wait until it is fixed or restart the programme (usually at the risk of losing what you had just written), whereas when you save to the hard drive, you have this sold storage of memory that can hold all the information you need with room to spare. The brain is the same – when overloaded with information, it finds it difficult to process that information and goes misty and often just shuts down – usually with a large migraine in tow. Like a hard drive, our long-term memory becomes the storage for all the information that has passed through the working memory and become embedded. Our working memory, on the other hand, only has a limited capacity with a small bottleneck connecting it to the long-term memory – meaning, not all information will pass through from the working memory to the long-term memory. When we are overloaded with information, that means there is even less chance of the knowledge to move through the bottleneck (Lovell, 2020). When things become chunked together and repeated, this makes it much easier to store in the long-term memory, which means you are more likely to do things instinctively without overthinking because it is firmly embedded

Table 4.4 Flipped learning lesson plan

'Pre-work' – to be completed at home before the lesson	• Delivered before the start of a topic/week/lesson • Can be delivered as a pre-recorded tutorial/video/reading material, etc. • Departments should collaborate with the pre-work material to ensure consistency • Could be shared online via Microsoft Teams/blackboard/VLE • Students should acknowledge they have received the material • Can be tracked and monitored in various ways
Starter/discussion	• Discuss with the class about the 'pre-work' material. • Use this time to iron out any misconceptions • Use active teaching strategies to help encourage engagement with students – think, pair, share/post-it notes/higher level questioning • Students who have not completed the pre-material could use this time to go away and watch it/catch up with clear sanctions put in place for the future, as they are now unable to make the most of their contact time with their 'facilitator' and classmates
Tasks/create	• Create a poster/mind-map to show understanding • SOLO Taxonomy based tasks • Differentiation • Learning zones • Challenge tables • Lead learners could be used to 'teach' the topic to the weaker students • Small group tasks/Individual work
Reflection	• Assessment for learning • Peer assessment (Green/Pink Pen) • Verbal feedback
Review	• Assess work and make improvements • Purple Pen tasks

into your brain, like an actor learning lines to a play, the repetitive nature of learning helps to move the words and actions through to the long term memory. I still remember playing mouse number 1 in my primary school's rendition of A Muppets' Christmas Carol – my one solo line was 'our assets are frozen.'

A key start to helping reduce the cognitive load of our students is removing anything that could be considered redundant. Don't overload your students with information, as there isn't enough space in their working memories to take it all in. A good example of this is when you have text on your PowerPoint that you then read out aloud. By doing this, you are getting your students to do twice as much work – they are trying to process the words on your PowerPoint slide while also processing the words they can hear – both vying for the same working memory space. Another form of redundancy is when you present images and words that both communicate the same thing – you are again doubling up on the same information – keep it simple.

Metacognitive evaluation

Through continuous use of verbally discussing the learning process this helps students to understand and evaluate how they have learnt in that lesson. It also allows them to remember this process so when they are next in a situation where they have to use the same skills, they will remember these pathways in order to solve problems a lot quicker in future. At the start of a task give students enough time to ask themselves 'how am I going to tackle this?', are they confident in what they need to do? If not, give them the opportunity to talk through the different approaches they might take. Think about using these question prompts to help them think about their learning:

- What do I already know about this topic?
- Have I done a similar task like this before?
- What strategies did I use last time?
- Where should I start?
- How am I doing?
- What should I do next?
- Is this strategy working, or should I change it?
- What should I do when I don't know what to do?

Once they have completed the tasks, develop a culture of self-evaluation – how well did I do? What could I do differently next time? These are just a few strategies you could try out with your students to help develop their cognitive and metacognitive abilities as they enter the crucial stages of their brain growth.

Chapter Summary

- Piaget's four levels of cognitive development – sensorimotor, pre-operational stage, concrete operational stage, and formal operational stage.
- Importance of understanding how students' brains work.
- Build opportunities to embed learning into the long-term memory.
- Embed Retrieval Practice regularly into lessons.
- Accelerate cognitive development by creating challenges and taking students out of their equilibrium.
- Creating environments for cognitive apprenticeships to take place.
- Make learning visible through speaking the thought processes out loud.
- Be mindful not to overdo the cognitive load.

So, what does an 'outstanding' teacher do?

They understand that students' brains do not work the same way as adults and therefore create opportunities to model how the brain processes information when faced with a challenge. Using more opportunities for students to practice skills in a range of contexts allows them to understand how skills work and determine which skills are better suited for different tasks.

References

Akınoğlu, O., & Tandoğan, R. (2007). The effects of problem-based active learning in science education on students' academic achievement, attitude and concept learning. *Eurasia Journal of Mathematics, Science and Technology Education, 3*(1), 71-81.

Arnett, J. (2013). *Adolescence and emerging adulthood: A cultural approach*. New York: Pearson Education Inc.

Baker, L. (2020). Metacognition strategies. In J. Hattie, & M. Anderman (Eds.), *Visible learning guide to student achievement* (pp. 253-254). Abingdon: Taylor and Francis.

Clarke, S., & Hattie, J. (2018). *Visible learning: Feedback*. London: Routledge, Taylor & Francis Group.

Classroom Window. (n.d.). *Improve student learning and teacher satisfaction in one flip of the classroom*. Retrieved from Flipped Learning Networks. https://flippedlearning.org/wp-content/uploads/2016/07/classroomwindowinfographic7-12.pdf

Garner, B. K. (2008, March 1). *When students seem stalled*. ASDC. https://www.ascd.org/el/articles/when-students-seem-stalled

Jones, K. (2021). *Retrieval practice: Resource guide: ideas & activities for the classroom*. Woodbridge, UK: John Catt Educational Ltd.

Jones, K. (2019). *Retrieval practice: Research & resources for every classroom*. Woodbridge, UK: John Catt Education Ltd.

Karpicke, J. (2012). Retrieval-based learning: Active retrieval promotes meaningful learning. *Current Directions in Psychological Science, 21*(3), 157-163.

Lovell, O. (2020). *Sweller's cognitive load theory in action*. Woodbridge, UK: John Catt Educational Ltd.

Michael, J. (2006). Where's the evidence that active learning works? *Advances Physiology Education, 30*, 159-167.

Millar, S., Venville, G., & Oliver, M. (2014). Cognitive acceleration. In R. Gunstone (Ed.), *Encyclopedia of science education*. Dordrecht: Springer.

Murre, J. M. J., & Dros, J. (2015). Replication and analysis of Ebbinghaus' forgetting curve. *PLOS ONE, 10*(7). https://doi.org/10.1371/journal.pone.0120644

O'Dowd, D. K., & Aguilar-Roca, N. (2009). Garage demos: Using physical models to illustrate dynamic aspects of microscopic biological processes. *CBE Life Science Education, 8*, 118-122.

Pencil Case. (2021, February 5). Piagetian programs. https://pencilcase.org/visible-learning-john-hattie/piagetian-programs.

Piaget, J. (2001). *The language and thought of the child*. London, UK: Routledge.

Quigley, A., Muijs, D., & Stringer, E. (2018). *Metacognition and self-regulated learning*. London: EEF. https://dera.ioe.ac.uk/31617/1/EEF_Metacognition_and_self-regulated_learning.pdf.

Shayer, M. (2003). Not just Piaget; not just Vygotsky, and certainly not Vygotsky as alternative to Piaget. *Learning and Instruction, 13*(5), 465-485. https://doi.org/10.1016/S0959-4752(03)00092-6

Sherrington, T. (2019). *Rosenshine's principles in action*. Woodbridge, UK: John Catt Educational.

Shrestha, P. (2017, November 17). *Ebbinghaus forgetting curve*. Retrieved from Psychestudy. https://www.psychestudy.com/cognitive/memory/ebbinghaus-forgetting-curve.

Stevens-Fulbrook, P. (2020). *Vygotsky, Piaget and Bloom: The definitive guide to their educational theories with examples of how they can be applied*. Self-published, Paul Stevens-Fulbrook.

Tomsett, J. (2021). *Collins et al's cognitive apprenticeship in action: In action series*. Woodbridge, UK: John Catt Educational Ltd.

Van der Stel, M., & Veenman, M. (2014). Metacognitive skills and intellectual ability of young adolescents: A longitudinal study from a developmental perspective. *European Journal of Psychology of Education, 29*, 117-137. https://doi.org/10.1007/s10212-013-0190-5

Watanabe-Crockett, L. (2019). *Future-focused learning: Ten essential shifts of everyday practice*. Bloomington, IN: Solution Tree Press.

Willingham, D. T. (2008). What will improve a student's memory? *American Educator, 32*(4), 17-44.

5 The importance of feedback

Feedback is an interesting topic and one that many educators debate over – what is it? How to best give it? When to give it? I am sure we can all think about a time in our lives when we have received really useful feedback, but at the same time, I know we have all, at some point, received that piece of information that served absolutely no purpose. There is nothing worse than receiving feedback that either doesn't make sense or doesn't actually give you any practical advice on where to go next. Feedback should provide information on areas that may need some sort of improvement or adaptation to be more successful next time. For a long time, 'feedback' wasn't even a thing – students' work would be graded and stored and that would be it. Teachers would 'mark' work in a summative way, providing information regarding how a particular grade had been met, but never used as a form of direction or guidance. Not until Ruth Butler conducted a study in 1988 where she had three groups, group A received only a grade, group B received only a comment and group C received both a grade and comment (Butler, 1988). The results of this experiment showed that those that received only a comment made better progress than the other two groups due to the fact that students often see grades as final – meaning they pay very little attention to comments when a grade is involved – even positive comments.

A common misconception of providing feedback is a tick box exercise for when book scrutinies take place, and you often see lots of pointless and ineffective comments like saying what the student has done well, or the typical 'not good enough,' or 'needs more focus.' Neither of these will help a student the next time they have to conduct a piece of work. This type of marking merely emphasises the underachievement of students, causing low self-esteem and diminishing any motivation a student might have had before. Mistakes should be normalised and celebrated, making them a common part of the learning process. As Royce Sadler (1988) points out, feedback should be used to 'close the gap.' Here is where you are, here is where you need to be, here is how you get there. But even this is pointless if students do not understand how to read the feedback and act on the comments provided. As Clarke and Hattie points out, 'feedback given but not heard is of little use' (2018, p. 5). With a potential effect size of 0.73, it is important to understand how to provide students with effective feedback which focuses on the learning, not just on the task itself.

DOI: 10.4324/9781003264453-5

This acknowledgement of effective feedback is recognised by the Education Inspection Framework in which they state in their outstanding descriptors, 'Teachers provide pupils with incisive feedback, in line with the school's assessment policy, about what pupils can do to improve their knowledge, understanding and skills. The pupils use this feedback effectively' (Ofsted, 2019). The key here is how the pupils use the feedback – being an English teacher, I know how tedious and time-consuming marking work can be, especially as we get closer to the KS4 and 5 exams and we have coursework and mocks to mark. As part of an experiment I decided to set a timer to see how long it took to mark students' work – 2 hours for 15 top set students. Did they spend anywhere near this time reading my comments? No. This instantly showed me how pointless this was – I had wasted valuable time that could have been utilised in a much better way. Ofsted and other inspection bodies are not looking to see you have done pages and pages of marking – that doesn't tell them anything about your practice – it is what type of feedback you are giving and how your students are responding that is important. 'I used to think giving more feedback and better feedback was the answer [to improving education], and it's the exact opposite: How do teachers and students receive feedback? How do they interpret it?' (Sparks, 2018).

Feedback shouldn't be just a routine task added to the end of a completed piece of work, instead it needs to be carefully planned with time provided specifically for students to interpret the feedback. Without providing this time, then students will struggle to understand the feedback provided, and therefore continue to make the same mistakes moving forward. According to Hattie, there is no instructional fit for feedback. Teachers need to know the optimal form of feedback to provide the student. The feedback needs to be:

1. related to where they are in the learning cycle
2. what they already know and understand (prior learning)
3. how the feedback is connected to the purposes of learning (learning objectives)
4. reducing the gap between where they are and where they need to go (success criteria).

Alex Quigley (2013) suggested using five strategies when providing feedback: keeping it focused, modeling and scaffolding, targeting the feedback, giving effective oral feedback and giving peer feedback, as you can see in Table 5.1.

Feedback doesn't just need to be a 'formative' or 'summative' task, if done well, feedback should be embedded throughout the learning journey, not just left towards the end. With the right kind of feedback, you develop the skill of intervening sparingly, giving just enough to get students going (Wiliam, 2011). Hattie breaks feedback down into three levels:

1. Task based – this is about the content and surface level information.
2. Processing – how do they go about making strategic decisions of where to go next?
3. Self-regulatory – students are more involved in detection and assessing their own work.

When giving feedback, think about the type you are providing – is it task based, just checking the understanding of the students, process based, in which you are discussing the thought process behind making an answer, or self-regulation where you are encouraging students to think independently and learn how to move forward and improve. As you move through the different types of feedback, you begin to develop those HOT skills.

60 The importance of feedback

Table 5.1 Quigley's five strategies

Keep it focused	Try not to be too vague with the feedback – if there is a specific part of the success criteria that is missing from the work, let students know. Students often don't get full marks because they don't know how to improve their work, so pinpoint them in the right direction – is it their spelling? Punctuation? Facts? Language techniques?
Model and scaffold	Asking students to 'improve their work' and then giving them 20 minutes to do so is more likely to encourage 15 minutes of chatter and 5 minutes of attempting to make some changes to their original work. Instead, use this time to provide students with models and scaffolding for what you expect – examples of well-worked pieces so that they can compare their work, sentence starters and example on the board, so students see why their work wasn't deemed as good first-time round.
Target the feedback	Feedback should be individualised to each student, with specific, clear targets of how they need to improve. SOLO Taxonomy works well here because you can show students where they currently are, and what they are lacking to push them into the next bracket – are they multistructural at the moment? What do they need to include to push them into the relational bracket?
Effective oral feedback	While students are given the time to reflect and improve their work, this is an optimum time to go around and provide effective oral feedback – talking with your students on a one-to-one level, providing individualised and differentiated feedback through questioning.
Peer feedback	Introducing 'lead learners' is a great way to effectively use peer feedback. I will often pair my lead learners up with students who might be struggling, so that they can help provide support to their peers.

Task-based feedback

There have often been lots of discussions surrounding when to best give feedback – immediately or after a period of time? Verbally or written? If you listen to Wiliam and Leahy then it really 'comes down to the simple truth that the most effective feedback is just feedback that our students actually use in improving their own learning' (2015, p. 107). Kate Jones (2021) breaks the purpose of feedback down to these three things (Table 5.2).

With task-based feedback, you are providing initial feedback about the work at hand, focusing on whether or not information has been understood and learning has taken place. While this may be considered surface-level feedback, it is a great way of incorporating Assessment for Learning (AfL) strategies into the lesson. I find that verbal feedback is usually the technique I use to check this surface level of understanding, as the students receive this feedback in the moment rather than waiting until the end of the lesson to then write it

Table 5.2 Purpose of feedback

Understandable	Have students understood the feedback? Do they know what they need to do with the feedback to improve?
Helpful	Does the feedback help the students progress and move forward?
Actionable	Have you provided an opportunity for students to respond and act on the feedback?

down somewhere. As the updated guidelines of the OFSTED Education Inspection Framework (2019) points out:

> teachers present subject matter clearly, promoting appropriate discussion about the subject matter they are teaching. They check learners' understanding systematically, identify misconceptions accurately and provide clear, **direct feedback**. In doing so, they respond and adapt their teaching as necessary, without unnecessarily elaborate or differentiated approaches
>
> (2019)

I will often use resources such as Kahoot to quiz my students on their learning, which instantly provides them with their results, allowing them to see where they need to spend their focus when revising the topic. By using Kahoot, I can also pause between questions, especially ones where the majority of the class answered incorrectly, so that I can discuss why they got it wrong and what the correct answer is. In order to incorporate this with retrieval practice, I will also continually repeat the same quiz every now and then so that students begin to embed the information into their long-term memories.

Another technique I use for task-based feedback with the younger years is the 2 stars and 1 wish technique (Figure 5.1). This allows students to peer assess their work using the lessons

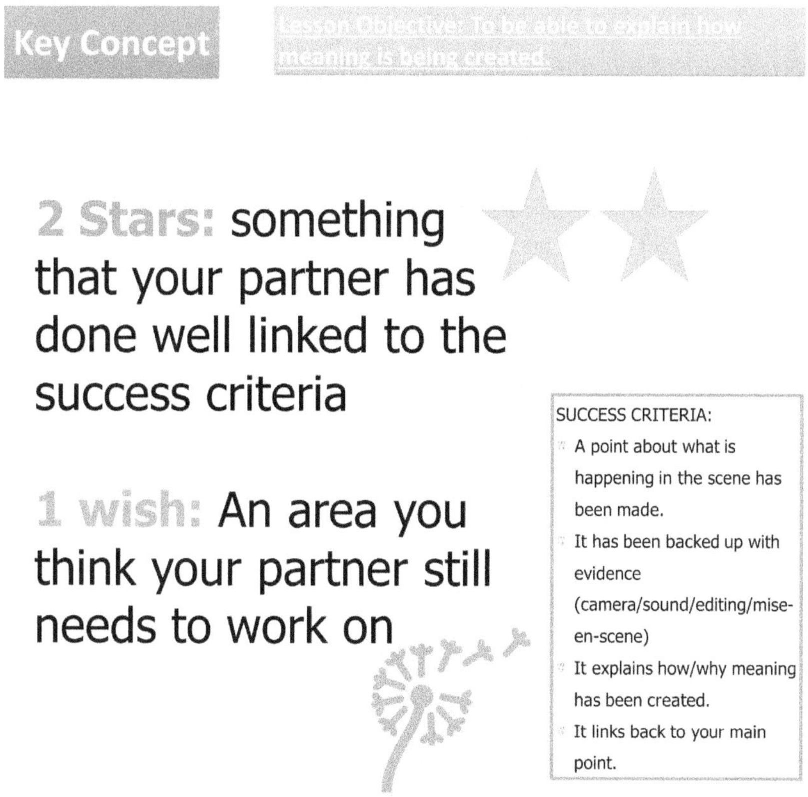

Key Concept — Lesson Objective: To be able to explain how meaning is being created.

2 Stars: something that your partner has done well linked to the success criteria

1 wish: An area you think your partner still needs to work on

SUCCESS CRITERIA:
- A point about what is happening in the scene has been made.
- It has been backed up with evidence (camera/sound/editing/mise-en-scene)
- It explains how/why meaning has been created.
- It links back to your main point.

Figure 5.1 Two stars and one wish

success criteria, providing feedback on what their partner has done well and what they need to do to improve. Having the success criteria on the board, I make sure they pick relevant statements rather than just comment 'I like your handwriting.' Making sure you plan this into your lesson effectively, means you can then give students enough time to respond and improve on the work that has just been marked.

Process-Based feedback

When providing feedback opportunities that focus on 'process,' you are giving your students the opportunity to explore their thought processes, and developing their ability to explore, sequence, and analyse information. Orlando (2015) and Halvorson (2014) both suggest that process-based feedback helps prepare students for future situations, making it clear that the outcome comes down to changes made in the process along the way – more understanding and focus on the process leads to better outcomes.

Linking back to my previous chapter, you can use questioning as a form of process-based feedback as well. Often you might ask a question that your students answer incorrectly – but this is a perfect time to normalise failure and show that mistakes allow us to learn from them. Thinking back to the IRE (initiate, respond, explore) structure I discussed in my chapter on questioning, use the explore part to question the response – why do they think this? How could they correct themselves? You want to get students to begin to internally evaluate their understanding, and normalise mistakes. Asking questions such as:

- Why might that answer be wrong?
- Why do you think you got to that answer?
- What information do you have available to get to the correct answer?
- What is the correct answer and why?
- What should you have done to get to the correct answer?

As Sadler (1983) pointed out, process feedback focuses on growth, allowing students to see and understand the journey rather than just being focused on the end goal and grade.

DIRT

One way of providing specific time for feedback is by introducing Dedicated Improvement and Reflection Time (DIRT) into your curriculum. This is a set time that you give to the students to be able to read, interpret and apply their feedback, making corrections to their work. As Beere and Gilbert point out in their book, 'The Perfect OFSTED Lesson' (2012) learning is a journey. Students need to know that it is not just about the end result, but that learning is a process that needs reflection and development – no one is perfect first time! A piece of work is not going to be a masterpiece in the first attempt. Encouraging DIRT throughout the learning phase allows students to stop and reflect along the way before it is too late. By providing formative feedback in the form of DIRT, students can actually

> In the 'score' advert, masculinity is represented in a more stereotypical manner. The male subject in the poster is identified as Propps' 'hero' due to his appearance and positioning. He is placed at a higher position than the rest of the subjects, which implies that he is higher in status, implementing a sense of patriarchy within the poster, which was a common issue in 1960's society. Additionally, the man is surrounded by provocatively dressed women which emphasizes that young men at the time were encouraged to be heterosexual. This is further evident through the tagline 'get what you've always wanted' which insinuates that every 'real' man's greatest desire is to be attractive to women. Moreover, the appearance of the women in the advert has links to voyeurism as they are being sexualized and objectified through their clothing – they act as mere accessories to the man. Although this representation of women was different compared to their previous 'good housewife' stereotype, being portrayed as sex symbols was becoming the new norm of 1960's society. **This may have been their representation in the 60's due to the media industry being male dominated, which would have resulted in these hegemonic ideologies.**
>
> *[UG]*
>
> *[Why do you think this was the representation in the 60s?]*
>
> On the other hand, the wrist watch advert conveys a very different message of masculinity. As it is a more recent advert, Van Zoonen's theory of alternative perceptions of gender according to changing times is proven here. Instead of being portrayed as a strong, powerful and aggressive man like in the score advert, the subject is shown to be more of a father figure. This may be viewed as uncommon as in previous years it was more conventional for females to adopt the role of a teacher than a man. This advert seems to be breaking those historical stereotypes. Additionally, there is no links to voyeurism within this advert and the advert is mainly centralized around the quality and preservation of the watch. The phrase 'you merely take care of it for the next generation' fits with the image on the poster as the man appears to be 'taking care' of his child (his next generation). However, there are still links to masculinity within this poster as the activity the man is taking part with his son in is perceived as something men would usually do – attending to a boat.
>
> *[What does it mean to be 'masculine' now? How has this changed over time?]*
>
> Well done, you make some valid points here and making good references to theory. Try to explain more about why our views of masculinity has changed - how has society's ideologies adapted the way men are represented in the media?
>
> 8/12

Figure 5.2 Example of student work (bold text)

see in specific detail how to improve their work, and are given the set time to do so. We do this by introducing the 'purple pen' in which any work students add are done using this colour so that it stands out and can easily be spotted when checking through their books. What is good about this is it doesn't have to be in their books either – during distance learning I used a lot of purple pen with the students when working online, getting them to instead just change the font of their text (Figure 5.2). By doing these exercises, it also provides the time and space for students to ask you questions, so that misconceptions can be cleared up.

When providing students with DIRT, I have also looked into ways of making students take more ownership over their work and their improvements. I wanted to create resilient learners who didn't just take on my feedback and made necessary improvements, but instead were challenged to think about the process more and work out their mistakes for themselves. This is when I came across feed-forward marking (Figure 5.3). As Dylan Williams points out 'feedback should be more work for the recipient than the donor.' In order to do this, I provide four key symbols for my students:

With this approach, the idea is to indicate to the students where they have either:

- Written something really impressive.
- Written something that doesn't make sense.
- Written something that is wrong.
- Written something with bad SPaG.

64 *The importance of feedback*

FEED-FORWARD SYMBOLS

You have written something that I really like! It is clear and at a high standard. You have made progress since your previous work. Your comments should follow: • I am really happy with this because… • I think you like my work because… • I have included… • I tried hard to… • I took on board my feedback and changes…. • I have progressed because…	There is something that isn't quite clear and needs explaining more. Your comments should follow: • I was trying to… • My intention was… • I wasn't sure about… • I was working on my… • I meant to say that… 
Something didn't quite make sense and needs re-drafting or correcting. Your comments should follow: • I struggled with… • I need to go back over… • I need to re-write this because… • The problem is… • I need your help with…	There is a SPAG error that needs fixing. Your comments should follow: • The correct spelling is… • The correct terminology is… • I forgot to… • I didn't include…

Figure 5.3 Feed-forward symbols

I first trialled this with my AS Media students, numbering the symbols in the margin and underlining the sections that they applied to. It meant that I could get through the marking much quicker as I was annotating with symbols as I went.

The start of the following lesson was then focused on students reflecting and critically thinking about their work. They had to look at where I had put the symbols, and then using the sentence starters on the board, they had to give themselves their own feedback. If they received a star, then they had to show why I thought it was a good line, if they received a question mark, they had to explain what they had written in more detail, an exclamation mark meant that something was incorrect or needed fixing and the full stop meant there was a grammatical error. While at first, my students were a little confused as this was a new approach for them, they eventually understood what was being asked of them. It also made them realise they had to be clear in their exam pieces as they would not be able to later explain to the examiner what they actually meant. Doing this was challenging them to think about what they were actually writing to ensure their explanations were clear. I was also teaching them the importance of drafting and checking for those mistakes and rectifying them.

For lower down the school, I think feedback provided during DIRT time needs to be much more structured and specific – while the above exercise is great to get students thinking and challenged, this is something that needs to be learnt and trained to do effectively.

Reassessment contract

Something I first came across on Twitter was the 'Reassessment contract.' When trying to create a culture of embracing mistakes and encouraging redrafting work, the reassessment contact allows students to take on board the feedback that has been given, and take their improvements into their own hands. It requires students to reflect on why their first piece of work was perhaps not to a higher standard and gets them to review what changes they are going to make to their learning to ensure their next attempt is going to be better. These can be created as an online form which can be submitted by students but usually follow this format (Table 5.3).

By reflecting and redrafting work, students are learning the importance of responding to constructive criticism and understanding the process that is taking place inside their own minds. By regularly embedding this practice into your curriculum, you develop this process so that students become faster at internalising their work, redrafting as they go to ensure the work, they are providing is at the best quality it can be. It gets students to start questioning themselves as to whether or not their work is hitting the success criteria, or whether more time and reflection are needed. Eventually, you build up your student's self-efficacy so that they no longer need to wait for your feedback but instead begin to become self-regulatory.

Table 5.3 Reassessment contract

Student's Name:	
Name of assignment:	
Reasons for needing to reassess:	School-based activities taking priority
	Job/work commitments
	Struggled to understand the task/material
	Procrastination
	Heavy course load
	Didn't study
	Silly mistakes
	Other
Explain the reasons for the boxes checked above.	
What activities will you undertake to ensure a better grade?	Revisit my notes
	1-2-1 session with teacher
	Revise the topic
	Do wider reading around the topic
	Use a thesaurus to improve my vocabulary
	Use the success criteria to ensure I am including on the necessary information
What date will my new completed assessment be done?	

66 *The importance of feedback*

Effective feedback should be targeted to students, in order to meet their level of skill or expertise. There is no point in giving self-regulation feedback to a novice. A novice requires feedback at the task level – about the basics. But, you then want to build on that – to develop those skills so that you provide students with the means to become more independent and so eventually, they are able to self-regulate.

Self-regulatory feedback

Encouraging self-regulation and self-assessment takes a much deeper understanding of their overall learning, as mentioned previously, it is something that needs to be built and developed. But introducing this as early as possible in the learning journey will allow students to grow the ability to be evaluative and become more self-efficient (more on this in my next chapter). When students have mastered the task and understand the process they have been through to get to where they are, the next step is to begin evaluating their success – critically thinking about their work and where they need to go next to make it better.

Some of the ways I get my KS4 and KS5 students to do this is by getting students to use the exam mark schemes and provide them with a range of examples. I ask my students to rate them from best to worst, using comments from the mark scheme to justify their reasons. Once we have established which pieces are the best and why, I get them to then reflect back on their own work, self-assessing and then redrafting before submitting their final pieces for me to mark. The purpose of self-regulatory feedback is to focus on 'Where am I going next?'

Another task-based activity to get my students to do to reflect on their learning is by getting them to RAG [Red (dark), Amber (bold), Green (light)] the topics we have covered (Figure 5.4). This is a great and visual way of seeing which topics students need more support with, it is also great as a

Media Studies Revision RAG

	I can recognise the different features of a magazine.	I can explain why they are important	I can analyse the use of colours - explaining the effect they have on the audience.	I know the different audience demographics	I can identify the different audience psychographics	I can explain how a magazine appeals to different audiences
	Yes	yes	yes	Fairly confident	not confident	yes
	yes	yes	yes	Fairly confident	Fairly confident	yes
	yes	yes	yes	Fairly confident	Fairly confident	yes
	yes	yes	yes	yes	fairly confident	yes

Figure 5.4 Student RAG task

revision tool as students can clearly see and self-regulate which topics they need to revise more for. In the below example, I can clearly see there is a pattern forming with my students' understanding of audiences, and so I know that I need to go back over this unit in more detail to help build their confidence.

Entry and Exit cards are also a great way for students to feedback to you to show how much they have understood from the lesson. As we use SOLO Taxonomy, I will often finish my lesson with the differentiated learning outcomes and get students' feedback on where they think they are based on the task they have just completed.

At the start of each term, we get our students to reflect on their current grades and the topic they have just been studying. This gives students the opportunity to look at their current grade in line with their target grade – how close are they? What steps do they need to take to ensure they succeed in reaching their targets? Getting students to set themselves SMART targets (Specific, Measurable, Achievable, Relevant, and Time-Bound), means that students are not just putting in vague goals, but actually thinking about how they are going to achieve these goals, how will they measure the impact between now and term 2 (Figure 5.5)?

In summary, there are plenty of ways of providing students with meaningful and effective feedback at all three levels. By covering task, process, and self-regulation, you are equipping your students with the ability to deal with tricky situations in the future (Table 5.4). They will

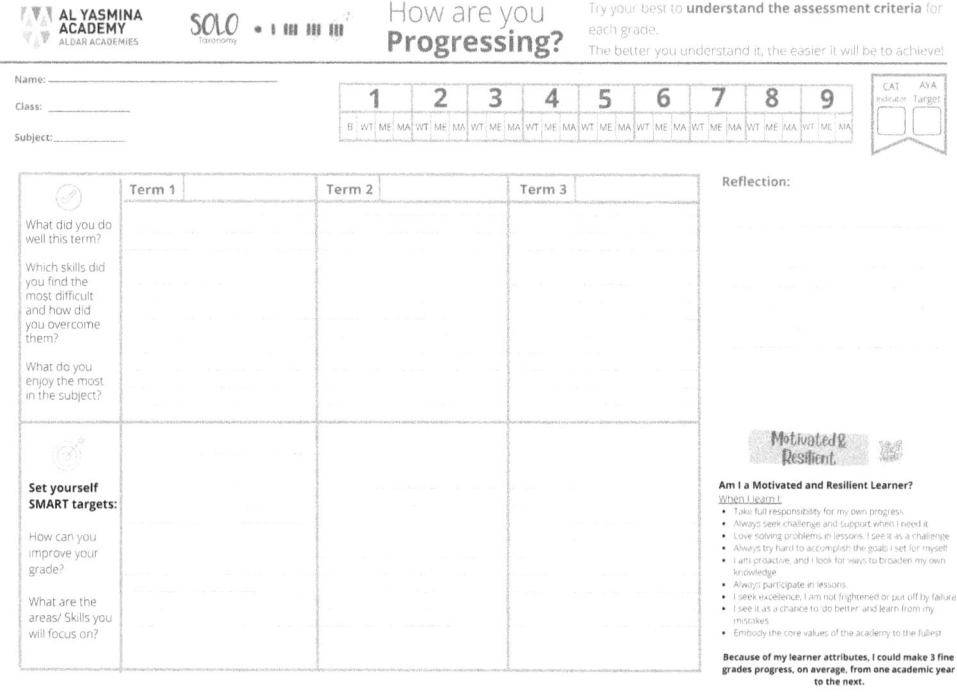

Figure 5.5 Student review

(This resource was created by a colleague of mine, Maie Salah Mansour, used with our students at Al Yasmina Academy, Abu Dhabi.)

68 The importance of feedback

Table 5.4 Feedback examples

	Task	Process	Self-Regulation
Re-teaching certain parts of the learning	2 stars and 1 wish – What do you mean by ….? Can you develop that a little?	Extended writing	Feed-forward symbols	Checking the success criteria/ using the mark scheme independently	What mark have you given yourself? Why? What do you need to include to get a better grade?
Quizzes	Peer assess marking	Correction starter/plenary	Verbal questioning – how did you work out the correct answer? How did you know it was incorrect?	Setting goals	What do you think your strengths and weaknesses are? What can you do to make sure you don't make the same mistakes again?
Plenaries	What have you learnt so far?	Giving the answer and asking what the question is.	Who has the correct question? Why do we think that is correct?	Feed-forward to teachers	Provide opportunities for students to inform your teaching – Was there a part of the learning that I didn't make clear? What area do you need me to go back over?
		Creating success criteria together	Why is it important to have success criteria? Does it need to be in a specific order? How can we put it into order? What are your reasons for ….?		
		Matching activities – finding relationship Analysing good examples/comparing different examples	Why did you add those together? Does it still work if I add ….? What grade would you give this? Why? How can it be made better? Have they forgotten anything? What are the strengths/weaknesses?		
		Redrafting	How could you change this to make it clearer?		

begin to internalise those questions, thinking about the process in order to ensure their final outcome is as strong as possible. Just to give you some more example, here are some other aspects you could include into your curriculum for the different stages:

Group feedback

As I mentioned earlier, being an English teacher, marking can often become very time-consuming. After conducting my timing experiment, I begin to research ways of making my feedback more effective for students but also less demanding for me – when I say this, I don't mean cutting corners – as teachers, we have to find ways to work SMART not necessarily work more. In Jones (2021), Dylan Williams breaks down marking into his 'Four Quarters' in which teachers should mark 25% of students' work in detail while skimming through 25%. Students should then be encouraged to self-assess 25% of their work and the final 25% should be peer assessed – with the support and guidance from the teacher.

One of the areas I looked into was the power of whole-class feedback. As Adam Riches (2021) points out, this is a highly effective and efficient way of having an impact on 'students' progress and, just as importantly, on teacher workload.' Often, by the time I have got to my tenth book, I notice I am writing the same comments, clearly seeing a pattern in the misconceptions my class may have had – why write this 10, 15, 20 times when I could just do it the once for all students to see? Here is an example of how a colleague of mine, Jancke Dunn (@awaken_english) uses whole-class feedback with her KS4 class (Figure 5.6):

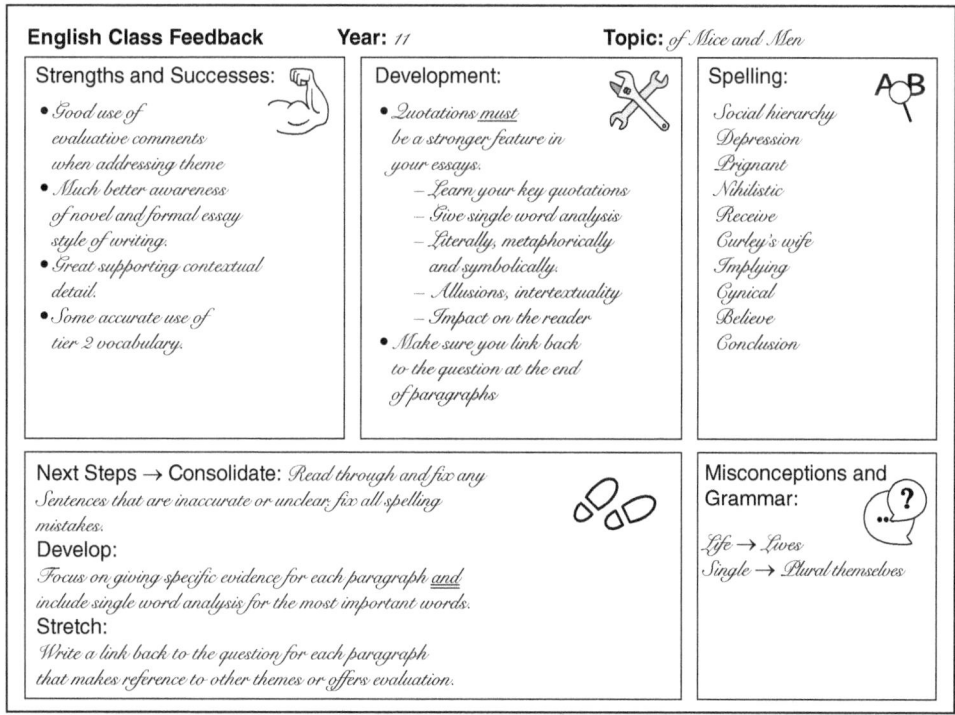

Figure 5.6 Group feedback

The importance of feedback

By using templates like this, you can show the class what is coming out as a success across the work being assessed, but also where the majority of issues are. I particularly like the spelling section as you often find it is the same words repeatedly being misspelt, so by modelling this through the Whole Class Marking (WCM), you are making them aware of what they need to practice. While some argue that WCM is less personal or individualised, it is still a useful tool when formatively marking, to help cover the key issues as a class. You can then allow students the time to go back over the work and make any amendments needed.

Feedback mats

Other ways I have looked into cutting down how long it takes to mark, while still making it effective for students is through creating a feedback mat (Figure 5.7):

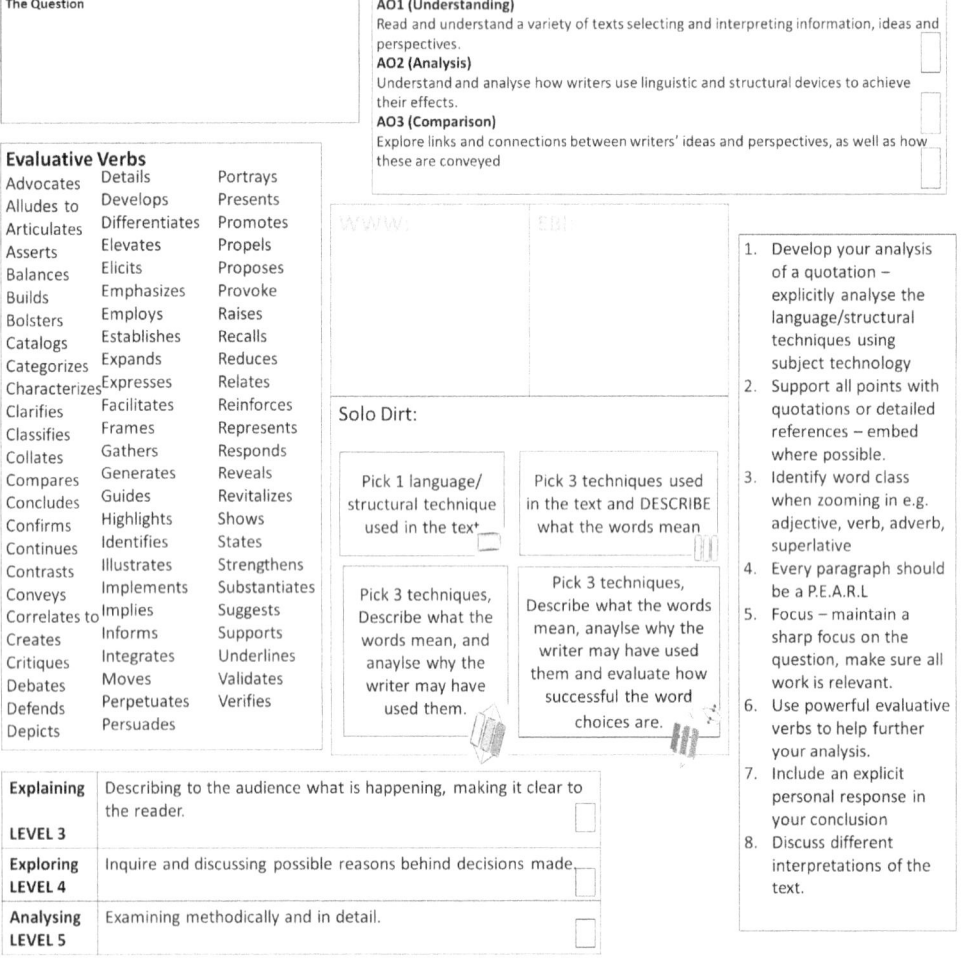

Figure 5.7 Feedback mat

I used this mat with my KS4 class when we were practicing for the IGCSE English Language exam. I used the evaluative verbs as a reminder to my students that they should be developing their vocabulary. I would highlight the verbs they had used in their answer as a way of showing them not to keep using the same ones over and over again. Often, I would only be highlighting the word 'shows' – a real visual eye-opener for my students when they weren't being adventurous with their words. I would then use a green highlighter on the right-hand side to show what the student had done well, such as 'support all points with quotations' and a pink highlighter for the areas that they had missed – usually the 'zooming' in on specific words in the quotes. I would tick which of the success criteria they had hit from the mark scheme, so they could see where they need to go next, as well as include a personalised 'WWW' (what went well) and 'EBI' (even better if). They would then have a go at the DIRT task based on the SOLO Taxonomy criteria. I found this useful as highlighting definitely takes a lot less time than writing, and it also meant that students could see exactly where in the text they would need to go back over to improve.

Teacher feedback

A sign of an outstanding teacher is one who is not afraid to request feedback on their own teaching and the impact they are having in the classroom. It always amazes me that so many people think that once they have completed their qualifications, they are done with learning. It is so easy to say 'I am the expert' because I have so many letters after my name – but even as an 'outstanding' teacher, I assure you – I am not an expert. I am constantly learning, adapting, reflecting, and evaluating. In an article written by Brooks, Huang, Hattie, Carroll, and Burton (2019), it is said that 'Items pertaining to feed forward (improvement-based feedback) were reported by students as most helpful to learning.' Students find it useful when we guide them to what they need to do to improve and get better – why would we not want that for ourselves?

So often, we are given a curriculum map at the beginning of the year, told when the student assessments will be (usually in line with whole school data drops and reports), creating the difficult task of fitting all content in, ready for the assessments so that we can move on to the next topic. So easily, the school year can become a complete whirlwind and there never seems to be enough time to deviate or add anything new into the mix. So many times, I have spoken to teachers who have said 'oh I would love to teach (insert topic), but I just don't have the time!' – but when planned properly, with feedback and development at the forefront of all teachers' minds, there can definitely be enough time. Workload can be significantly reduced when time is given to plan effectively and use feedback to inform future planning.

We speak to students every single day, but when do we ask them to give feedback to us? Often the students' voice is diminished due to time limitations. By giving students the opportunity to provide feedback and allow their voices to be heard, you begin to get that real sense of visible learning.

Some of the easiest ways I have incorporated this into my lessons is by asking my students to give me a 'WWW' and 'EBI' and stick it on my whiteboard as they leave.

They can do this anonymously – I usually turn my back while they go up and stick them on the board, and they often have a good giggle about rearranging them so I can't guess who wrote it.

Other times, I have used 'exit' cards with the questions – 'What did your teacher help you learn today?' and 'What could your teacher do differently to help you understand better?' Wallace and Kirkman (2017) also suggest the following questions for your students:

- Which part of the topic did you find most interesting? Why?
- Which part did you find least interesting? How could I make it more interesting for another class?
- What aspects of the topic do you remember best? Why do you think that is?
- Which activities or tasks helped you to learn best?
- Which parts of the topic did you struggle to understand?
- Was there an aspect of the topic you wish you'd had more time to explore?
- If you were going to teach this topic to someone else, how would you do it?

Verbal feedback

There is a lot of debate surrounding giving verbal feedback, and whether or not it can be just as effective as written feedback. The Education Endowment Foundation published a report in 2016 (Elliot et al., 2016) which explored how many hours teachers were typical spending on providing feedback, with the typical teacher spending around nine hours a week on marking pupils' work – not dissimilar to the 2 hours I took to mark my year 11 books. And again, there was little evidence to really show whether or not this was having a positive impact on the students.

There seems to be some scepticism around verbal feedback as it is very hard to evidence when it has taken place. With many teachers having to face book scrutinies, it is not always easy to look back through students' work and pinpoint when this type of feedback was given. However, Katie Kerr's research actually showed that students respond better to the verbal feedback as they see it as being more meaningful and focused conversations based on their personal targets and goals (Kerr, 2017). As Hattie and Clarke point out in their book, verbal feedback within lessons is so important as students are getting in the moment responses rather than waiting until after the learning has taken place. In 2019, the University College London (UCL) teamed up with Ross McGill from @TeacherToolkit to take on research for the Verbal Feedback Report. For their research, they worked with 13 teachers across 8 different schools in the UK, focusing specifically on the impact of verbal feedback in Key Stage 3 – in particular, disadvantaged students. During the research, their findings showed that verbal feedback was a 'complex series of refinements to practise' and that 'when accompanied by a reduction or removal of written forms of feedback, does not negatively affect either the engagement or attainment of students' (McGill, 2019, p. 6). At the start of the project, the UCL equipped teachers with training and a range of resources to help build their confidence in using verbal feedback in the lesson.

According to the report, these were some of the more popular approaches taken by teachers:

- Questioning techniques
- Live marking
- Increased 1:1 interaction
- Modelling of responses
- Whole class feedback discussed together
- Peer and/or self-assessment
- Use of praise
- Using more zonal marking to reduce written feedback

While many of the teachers found it hard to reduce the written feedback to begin with the findings of the research concluded that, when applied accurately, verbal feedback has a positive impact on engagement, attainment and progress, student-teacher relationships, workload, and mental health. As reported, 'verbal feedback is something that teachers can learn to do, can get better at doing and then can have an increasing effect on their students' (McGill, 2019, p. 29).

Some strategies that can be used to help more verbal feedback in lessons can be seen below:

Cold calling

As mentioned before, cold calling is a fantastic way of engaging students in classroom discussions. To avoid students from being passive and silent, cold calling allows you to question even the most reserved students, providing instant feedback on their answers. When using cold calling, you would pose a question to the class followed by silence to allow students time to think. After an appropriate time (remember what I said before about jumping in too quick), pick a student to answer and follow it up with feedback, then pick another student to elaborate or challenge the answer given. This technique is not designed to catch students out, but instead to make your questioning and feedback inclusive of all students. To formulate a discussion. As mentioned in my previous chapters, you want to get students thinking, and using retrieval practice strategies to help build their confidence. As Dan Willingham points out in his book, 'Why Don't Students Like School' (2021) if students don't think, then they cannot learn, as memory is the remaining part of thought. I relied a lot on this technique during distance learning, as my students were very content with keeping their cameras and microphones firmly switched off. By using cold calling, I sent the message to my students that I expected all to participate, but it also meant that I could provide instant and meaningful feedback to them while they were online.

Pose, pause, pounce, bounce (PPPB)

This technique is by no means a new strategy, but it is still a very effective way of incorporating AfL into lessons, as shown by Ross Morrison McGill in his @Teachertoolkit. This technique is broken down into four sections:

1. Pose - start off with a reflective question that needs time to think about.
2. Pause - allow students time to think and gather their thoughts. Ask students to remain silent and re-think, check they are happy with their answers, and hold it for as long as possible.

3 Pounce – pick a student to respond to the question (there may be some guiding to help said student).
4 Bounce – once your first student has answered, immediately ask your second student what their thoughts are on the first student's answer. Continue this for as long as possible.

Here you are effectively getting students to give peer feedback on each other's answers – they are evaluating the strength of each other's answers and exploring ways of making it better.

Mini whiteboards

Mini whiteboards are a great way of including quick AfL into lessons – checking students understanding. But this technique also allows you to uncover any misconceptions and errors – providing on-the-spot feedback to students when they get an incorrect answer. Again, it gives you the opportunity to incorporate some PPPB by getting students to peer assess each other's answers.

Zonal marking

When you use zonal marking, you reduce what is written in a student's book, and replace instead with marking codes. Just like the feed-forward symbols, I showed earlier on in this chapter. One I like to use when giving verbal feedback is simply writing VF in the margin of students' books to showcase that feedback was given during discussion. Sometimes I might ask my students to answer my verbal feedback/questioning by responding just next to my VF mark.

Four questions

Stephen Dinham (2014) suggests, when giving feedback to focus on these four questions:

1 What can the student do?
2 What can't the student do?
3 How does the student's work compare with that of others?
4 How can the student do better?

Dinham suggests that when teachers provide answers to these four questions regularly, they are driving remediation and improving performance.

In the conclusion of the UCL report, it was stated that verbal feedback is not easy but it is something that teachers can learn to do, and as they get better at it, so does their increasing effect on student performance. When verbal feedback is done properly, then it does have a positive impact on engaging students and their overall performance, giving teachers more time to focus on their teaching and planning.

Chapter Summary

- Feedback is essential to show students how to progress.
- Feedback must be understood by students, otherwise, it is pointless.
- Feedback can be broken down into different stages – task based, process based, and self-regulatory.
- Feedback should inform the students about where they are, where they are going, and how to get there.
- Teachers should encourage student's voice.
- There are a range of ways of providing students with feedback including verbal feedback.

So, what does an 'outstanding' teacher do?

They don't waste time with unnecessary feedback – they use it to inform their own planning but also to provide students with the tools to be self-reflective and know how to make improvements. Using a range of feedback techniques, teachers get students to think about their learning to ensure lessons are learnt and mistakes are rectified.

References

Beere, J., & Gilbert, I. (2012). *The perfect Ofsted lesson*. Bancyfelin: Independent Thinking Press.

Brooks, C., Huang, Y., Hattie, J., Carroll, A., & Burton, R. (2019). *What is my next step? School students' perceptions of feedback*. Retrieved from Frontiers in Education. https://www.frontiersin.org/articles/10.3389/feduc.2019.00096/full

Butler, R. (1988). Enhancing and undermining intrinsic motivation: The effects of task-involving and ego-involving evaluation on interest and performance. *British Journal of Educational Psychology*, 58(1), 1-14.

Dinham, S. (2014, May 14). *Feedback on feedback*. Retrieved from Teacher Magazine website. https://www.teachermagazine.com/au_en/articles/feedback-on-feedback

Elliot, V., Baird, J., Hopfenbeck, T. H., Ingram, J., Thompson, I., Usher, N. ... Coleman, R. (2016). *A marked improvement? A review of the evidence on written marking*. https://d2tic4wvo1iusb.cloudfront.net/documents/guidance/EEF_Marking_Review_April_2016.pdf?v=1629121916

Halvorson, H. (2014). *The key to great feedback? Praise the process, not the person*. Retrieved from 99U. http://99u.com/articles/19442/the-key-to-great-feedback-praise-the-process-not-the-person

Hattie, J., & Clarke, S. (2018). *Visible learning: Feedback*. London: Routledge, Taylor & Francis Group.

Jones, K. (2021). *Wiliam & Leahy's five formative assessment strategies in action (in action series)*. Woodbridge, UK: John Catt Educational Ltd.

Kerr, K. (2017). Exploring student perceptions of verbal feedback. *Research Papers in Education*, 32(2), 1-19.

McGill, R. (2019). *UCL Verbal Feedback Project Report 2019*. Retrieved from UCL Access and Widening Participation. https://www.ucl.ac.uk/widening-participation/sites/widening_participation/files/2019_verbal_feedback_project_final_4_print.pdf

Ofsted. (2019, July 23). *Education inspection framework*. Retrieved from GOV.UK website. https://www.gov.uk/government/publications/education-inspection-framework/education-inspection-framework

Orlando, J. D. (2015). *Is praise undermining student motivation?* Retrieved from Faculty Focus. http://www.facultyfocus.com/articles/educationalassessment/praise-undermining-student-motivation/

Quigley, A. (2013, October 12). *Dirty work* [Blog Post]. https://docs.google.com/document/d/1hZPT8ksC1_jeGugGnBpBdDgRwbIH7phgdUh1D8IbSgO/edit

Riches, A. (2021, April 19). *Whole-class feedback: Practical tips and ideas*. Retrieved from Headteacher Update. https://www.headteacher-update.com/best-practice-article/whole-class-feedback-practical-tips-and-ideas-assessment-pedagogy-teaching-marking-1/236434/

Sadler, D. (1983). Evaluation and improvement of academic learning. *Journal of Higher Education*, 54(1), 60-79.

Sadler, R. (1988). Formative assessment and the design of instruction systems. *Instructional Science*, 18, 119-44.

Sparks, S. D. (2018, June 20). *Getting feedback right: A Q&A with John Hattie*. Retrieved from Education Week website. https://www.edweek.org/leadership/getting-feedback-right-a-q-a-with-john-hattie/2018/06

Wallace, I., & Kirkman, L. (2017). *Best of the best: Progress*. Carmarthen, UK: Crown House Publishing.

Wiliam, D. (2011). *Embedded formative assessment*. Bloomington, IN: Solution Tree Press.

Wiliam, D., & Leahy, S. (2015). *Embedding formative assessment: Practical techniques for K-12 classrooms*. West Palm Beach, FL: Learning Sciences International.

Willingham, D. T. (2021). *Why don't students like school? A cognitive scientist answers questions about how the mind works and what it means for your classroom*. Hoboken, NJ: Jossey-Bass.

6 Self-efficacy – Developing staff and students

Have you ever been to a CPD session when the Senior Leadership Team uses the analogy of students' emotions with a full bottle of fizzy drink? They talk through a teenager's average day, one full of impulsive emotions and feelings, and each time something challenging gets in their way, they shake the bottle. By the end of the hypothetical day, they have shaken it up so much, you know what will happen if you take that lid off – try it out – I guarantee nobody will be brave enough to unscrew the cap. I like this activity because it demonstrates how young children try to contain their emotions, bottling them up, not knowing how to deal with them – is it any wonder that sometimes they burst, lash out, explode? It is so easy to write that off as a behaviour issue – punish them for having an emotion, give them a detention for not knowing how to express their emotions correctly – but what does that achieve? The real issue is much more important – why do they feel that way, and how can we teach them to deal with those stresses and anxieties? A lot of grown adults are not able to control their emotions at times (ever stumped your toe on a corner?!), so how can we expect children to, if we don't give them the tools?

Self-efficacy is by no means a new concept, and for all you psychologists out there, you will know that it was first coined by Albert Bandura in the 1970s. Self-efficacy was seen as being how well a person believed in their ability to deal with challenging situations. In other words, when we face something unexpected or out of our control, it is our personal belief whether or not we can overcome these situations. This affects children and adults daily, and if we are not taught how to process and execute a plan of action, then we often just fail at the challenge at hand. We all have that little voice in our heads that says, 'you can't do this,' 'just give up,' 'there is no point.' I know I have that voice regularly even in adulthood on a regular basis – and perhaps that is because I wasn't taught the tools when I was at school – but it is never too late to begin developing those skills. Of course, embedding it from a young age is much more effective than in adulthood, but you can begin to change that mindset at any point. So, this chapter is dedicated to supporting both staff and students in developing those tools of self-efficacy and resilience.

Hands down, the last two years of COVID-19 have definitely challenged us and our self-efficacy – dealing with constant uncertainty and having to totally revamp our whole teaching practice, stepping out of our comfort zone, and learning how to teach in this new environment. Firstly – you are amazing! We are amazing! It is so easy to get lost in the day-to-day

DOI: 10.4324/9781003264453-6

worry and pressure of trying to 'get it right' – but improving self-efficacy is about saying it is ok to get it wrong. In situations like this, I love to remind myself of the amazing Carol Dweck (2017) and her power of 'yet' – we may not have got there 'yet' but we will. To build our meta-cognitive ability to develop our self-efficacy, we must focus on those key skills of perseverance and resilience, building our confidence, to know we can overcome these challenges that we face. I remember being in Abu Dhabi during the first lockdown – March 2020, we all went to online learning. All of a sudden, I had a much-reduced timetable, I was still worried that exams were going ahead (they had not been cancelled at this point), I had students refusing to turn on their cameras, I had students just not turning up for the lessons – I felt like a failure. How on earth was I going to do my job and do it well, and achieve the same outcomes as I was doing before? I think we teachers tend to put so much more pressure on ourselves – we will stay up all night chasing students for work, a lot of us were still responding to messages at 2 am. We do it because we care, and we want our students to succeed – but again, they rely so much on us, how are we actually helping them? Despite these anxieties, however, we did get through that first lockdown. We learnt about new technologies – Kahoot, Concept Board, Stormboard, Polly, Online Whiteboards – all these tools were always there, but we were never in a situation where we used them. We began redefining education and learning. We began growing our skills, and that of our students. We were growing in our confidence in how to teach online – we began to believe in ourselves and develop our self-efficacy.

So let us dig a little deeper into exploring what 'Self-Efficacy' actually is and begin looking at strategies to help develop it both in our lessons and with our teachers as well. Those of you who already know about Bandura, then please humour me here as I break down my interpretation of his theory. In his books, Bandura divides self-efficacy into four key areas, which we are going to explore now.

Performance outcomes: Mastering experiences

Whenever we take on new experiences, whether in childhood or as an adult, we grow through our successes. If we are successful, then we are more likely to do it again. Think about when you first start learning to ride a bike (I have just been through this with my own daughter), it is scary, your stabilisers come off and you are expected to just peddle and balance. Sounds easy, right? Wrong – this first attempt almost always ends with a fail – as soon as you realise Mum and Dad are no longer holding on, you take that look back to check, lose all control and topple over. If you are lucky, you topple onto a soft landing, like grass, if you're not then you are guaranteed a bloody knee or elbow! After this attempt, could I get my daughter back on? No – she saw this as a failure and didn't believe she could succeed. Her self-efficacy was too low to have that belief in herself. However, after lots of tears, tantrums, refusals to ever ride a bike again, and 'I can't do it!,' we eventually got her back on. Did she fall off again? Of course! But each time, she got a little bit more resilient, a little bit braver, and then she started to ride. Not far – still working on that one, but enough to have the belief in her ability to succeed. When she falls off, she doesn't cry anymore, she instantly picks herself up and tries again. As Bandura tells us, success creates a strong and sturdy belief in our self-efficacy (Bandura, 1997). What my daughter has learnt from this experience is that it is ok if it didn't go right the first time. She knows that things take practice and time and that if she falls off, then all she needs to do is pick herself up and go again. This is the same with our students and teachers – learning isn't a straight and easy road, there are bumps along the way, and the more successful you are at dealing with those bumps, the more belief you will have in your ability to deal with the next bump, and the one after that.

This links nicely to James Nottingham's Learning Pit (2017), in which he explores the ways to master a deeper understanding within learning and celebrate those 'Eureka' moments. So many of us give up when we hit the bottom of the 'pit' feeling like the challenge at hand is too difficult for us – ever tried the couch to 5k or started one of those 30-day workout challenges? If you are anything like me, you get to about week 3 and give up. But for self-efficacy to grow, the bottom of the pit is the crucial moment in developing that belief. Once you get over the hurdle and begin working your way back out of the pit, you look back with pride – you have overcome a challenge (regardless of what it is) and you have succeeded. This means the next time you are in that pit; you can remind yourself of how you overcame the challenge last time, you are more likely to be motivated to do it again (Figure 6.1). Having reminders of this on your displays are also a great way of encouraging students to be self-regulated (Figure 6.2).

A great way of building on success is by having discussions with your students. Establish what your students already know about a topic you are beginning – this will help you determine what level your students are at – are they pre-structural, unistructural, etc. Rather than expecting all students to start at the same level – which is more than likely just going to diminish a student's confidence if they are unable to achieve the task at hand, establish the

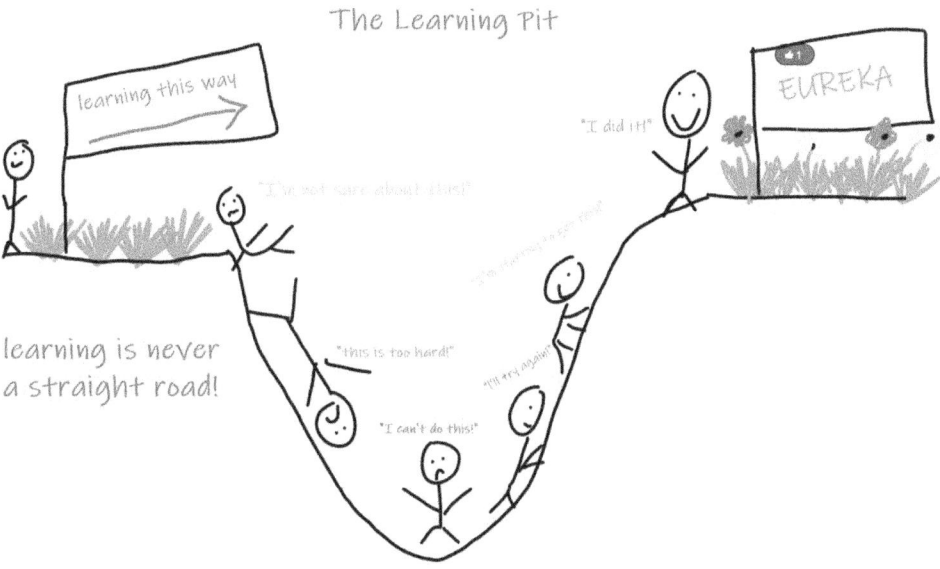

Figure 6.1 The learning pit

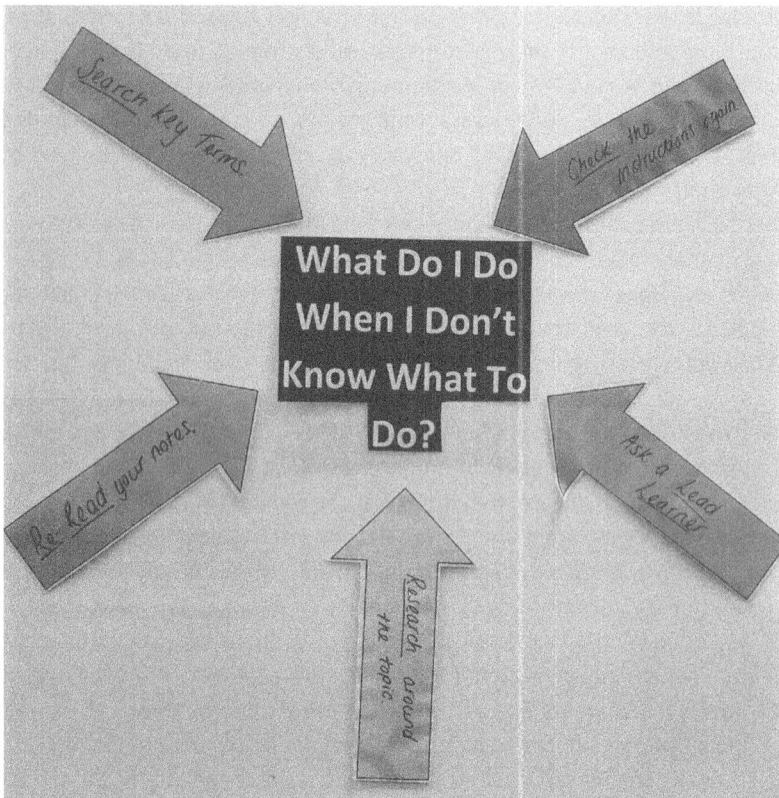

Figure 6.2 Display board

starting point. You could do this by getting them to use Pam Hook and Julie Mills' SOLO hand symbol (2011) (Figure 6.3).

A large factor behind building self-efficacy is getting over that 'fear of failure' as UC Berkeley Professor, Martin Covington discusses in his book *'The Will to Learn: A Guide for Motivating Young People'* (1999). People will do everything they can to avoid failure so that they can continue to feel worthy as Vicki Zakrzewski discusses in her article, *'How to Help Kids Overcome Fear of Failure'* (2013). This initial fear can potentially have a long-term impact if not overcome, as they will continue to live their lives avoiding any situation they deem too hard, or something they are not going to achieve. I am the same when it comes to Maths – I have a genuine fear of maths, I have told myself over and over again, if it is more than what I can count on my fingers, then I cannot do it – therefore, I don't even try. My mind literally blanks out and I stop processing information if numbers are involved. I clearly did not master my experiences in Maths when I was at school. I had an amazing maths tutor who was wonderful, who helped me achieve my C at GCSE but other than that, I hated maths – which continued into adulthood. This links to Robert Kegan and Lisa Lahey's really interesting article, *'The Real Reason People Won't Change'* (2001), in which they discuss the concept of 'competing commitments,' more specifically linked to the idea of change, but I think this concept still applies here. Often, we can be opposed to doing things because deep down our subconscious

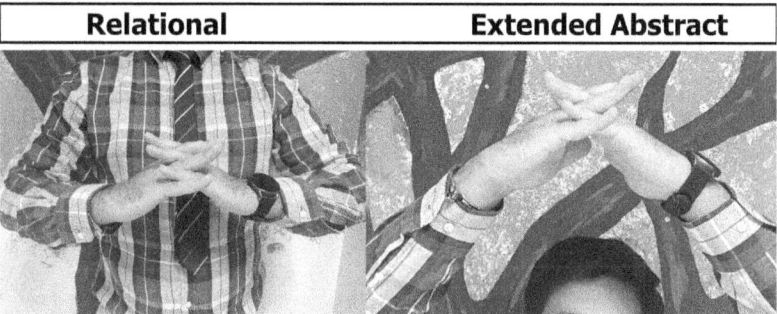

Figure 6.3 SOLO taxonomy symbols

is holding us back, we have competing commitments that we do not want to stray from. For example, when I was first asked to lead Innovation and STEAM, I was very reluctant, it didn't fill me with the excitement and passion other Teaching and Learning roles had and as a result, I was very slow with getting it set up. However, when digging deeper and exploring this more, I realised that my competing commitment was my fear of failing or being seen as not good in the role. I was worried because I associated innovation with science and technology, and therefore didn't think I could do it. But once I was able to realise and accept that this was a fear of mine, I was able to look at it from a different perspective, and as a result, I was able to work with students who had a passion for this area and we were able to run our first virtual Science Fair, Online MUN conference and run clubs such as Astrophysics and Coding Club. So, when staff and students seem reluctant or not getting involved, talk to them, try and determine what their competing commitment is, often this could be due to fear, which can stop even the most productive of people. Try to embed Carol Dweck's power of 'Yet' – building in that positive mindset. Part of the struggle is getting our students to believe that they have what it takes to be successful, even if they don't get it the first time around. Encouraging participation – getting people to be active and engaged will usually influence a person's level of self-efficacy. Active class participation is also correlated to having high critical and higher-level thinking skills. By using SOLO, you can differentiate

82 Self-efficacy – Developing staff and students

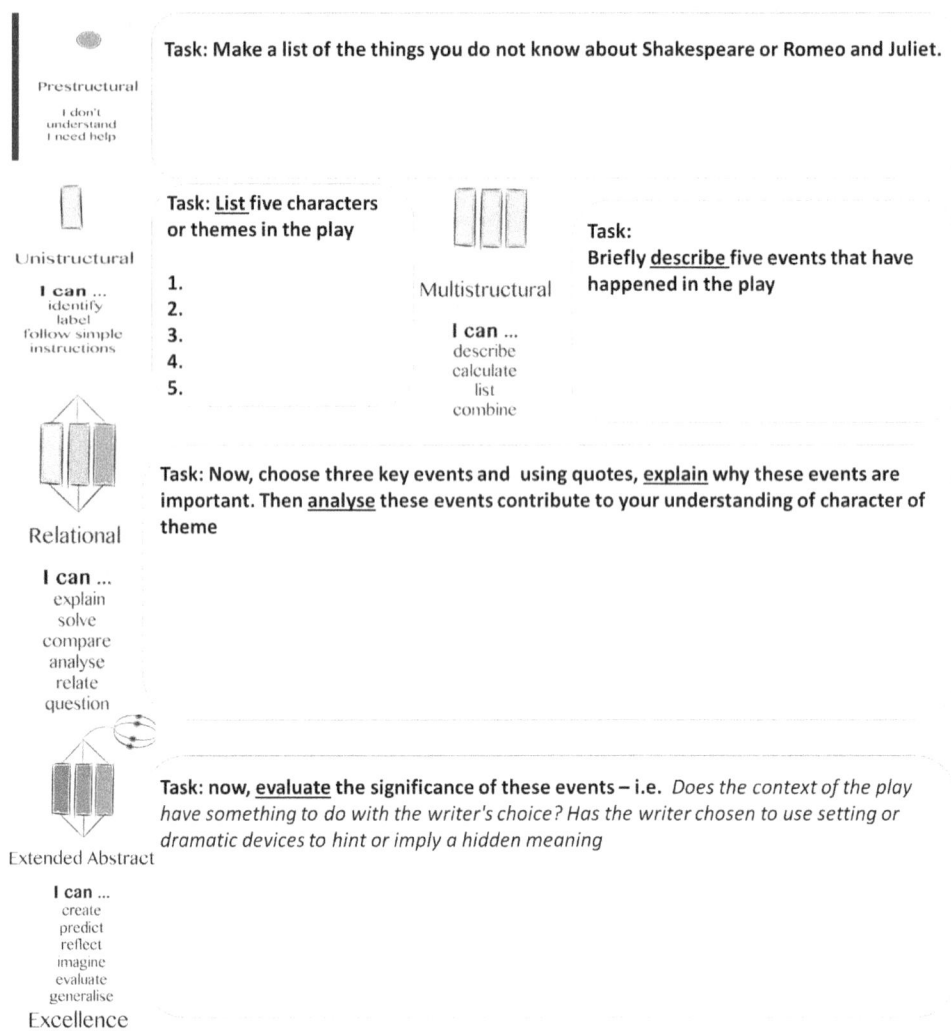

Figure 6.4 SOLO taxonomy tasks

the task so all students can participate at the level designed for them (Figure 6.4). It also gives them the chance to see what the next steps are so that they can build on their skills, to get to that next step.

One of the key ways of encouraging success is by creating a space where mistakes are ok, in fact, mistakes are part of that success. Manu Kapur (2008) discusses the idea of 'Productive Failure' in which it becomes part of the learning design where learners begin with generating and exploring representations and solution methods (RMS) in order to try and solve problems. This means the conventional instruction given by teachers is reversed, encouraging students to attempt to solve the problem before they receive clear instruction. By doing this, it leads to them making initial mistakes or failures, as their results are often mediocre. Once receiving the instruction, they can see where they went wrong and learn to solve the problem better.

Just watch *Count Down* when Rachel Riley starts doing the team's workings out on the board as they talk through their math problem. Even though she can do it in a blink, she still allows them to walk her through it – and more times than not, they see where they have gone wrong before she tells them. You can physically see the process taking place, as she allows them to have a go and then she models the correct answer. This is often useful in subjects like Maths and Science. I saw it work well during our extra-curricular Coding Club run by a student. She would often tell the class what it was they were going to try and achieve that day, allow them to attempt the coding themselves, using their intuition and previous knowledge, and then she would provide them with the correct instructions, so they were able to see where they went wrong and could then correct it. While initially there was 'failure,' that was part of the learning – through getting it wrong, they could see how to get it right. I have also used this technique with my BTEC Media classes, in which I told them what the outcome was – to design a new magazine, but I asked them to think about how they would get to that point – what did they need to do to finish with a successful magazine that their audience would want to read?

Having studied different research techniques, students had to apply their knowledge to this problem and work out what types of research would be the most beneficial in this situation (Figure 6.5). Once completed, we went through it as a class and discussed the varying

Figure 6.5 Lesson resource

options and discussed which ones would be the most appropriate, and why some of their ideas might not have worked as well as others.

In our school, we like to encourage DIRT (Dedicated Independent Reflection Time), in which students can have the time needed to reflect on their work, especially if they didn't achieve the grade they were hoping for.

Using 'pink for think' and 'purple for polish,' we encourage our students to redraft work. So many times, I have had a student throw a piece of work at me and tell me 'Finished,' and in their heads they are. That's it, end of the process – work is completed therefore they are done. But that mindset means if the work is final, then the grade is final. There is no mastering of skills there – there is just disappointment and confusion as to why they were not more successful. As Covington has explained, students tend to focus on that grade, if it is good, then they believe it is an inherent ability, and if poor, then it is purely inability – it is a very black-and-white concept to them. If they do not achieve the grade they want, they see it as a failure that cannot be avoided, instead of accepting and understanding the process of hard work and development. Lazarus and Launier (1978) add to this as they suggest that people who view themselves as unsuccessful and weakened by obstacles, will tend to give up when they face challenges and no longer participate in the activity.

We all know that the first thing a student does is look at the grade and then compares it with their friends – 'Miss, why did I only get a C when Louise got an A?' The same applies to teachers – 'why is my lesson only good and he got outstanding?' This goes back to my overarching point of this book – we learn through reflection, evaluation, and change. I won't delve into this too much as I have already discussed it in my previous chapter, but this just reinforces the importance of building success. It does not happen straight away. This is where the 'Reassessment Contract' works really well, in which students apply to redo their work as mentioned in my previous chapter. Using something like Google Forms, you get students to fill in a survey questioning them on what the reason might be that they didn't do as well as they hoped, and what strategies they plan to use to ensure their second submission is better. This allows students to reflect on their work, take ownership of their learning and address the reasons why they did not achieve so well the first time around. After owning their mistakes, they must explain how they plan to learn from this and showcase what they will do to improve next time around, to ensure they don't make the same mistakes. Students will quickly learn what their downfalls are, they will be able to use that to motivate themselves to improve and then learn from those mistakes the next time. Once they master the skills and make the required improvements, see their grades improve, and their self-efficacy will grow. And these techniques can be used in any year group – make happy mistakes!

Vicarious experiences: Social role models

The next key area in Bandura's Self-Efficacy theory is focused on the idea of having vicarious experiences. 'Learning would be exceedingly laborious, not to mention hazardous,

Self-efficacy – Developing staff and students 85

if people had to rely solely on the effects of their own actions to inform them what to do. Fortunately, most human behaviour is learned observationally through modelling: from observing others, one forms an idea of how new behaviours are performed' (Bandura, 1977, p22). By watching people similar to you succeed, it raises your own beliefs that you too have the capability to achieve that same success. When my daughter was learning to swim, she was afraid to jump straight in. One day, while we were chilling by the pool, a family came in with 2 small children – around 3 and 1. Both these children were so confident with the water they both jumped straight into the deep end – Dad was not worried in the slightest. He was confident that they both knew what to do, and just like that, they both emerged from the water and instinctively swam to the side to hold on. There was no panic or worry, these two children were confident and not afraid of the water. Because of this positive attitude, my daughter saw these children as role models, if they could do it then so could she – she was 2 at the time. And before I knew it, she just jumped straight in, and copied what the other children did, she turned around and swan to the side to hold on. I was shocked and amazed – something I had been trying to get her to do for months, was conquered in a matter of minutes by watching her peers and having that self-belief. Modelling is considered to be most effective with a child's direct peers (siblings, parents, teachers, friends) – they set the example. This same thing applies in a classroom – students are constantly watching each other as well as you, their teacher – everyone in that classroom is modelling. By being positive role models, you instil that confidence, they can see you and their peers succeed, and they want to as well. Not only this, but they also watch how each other deals with problems, and how they respond to any issues they face. According to Hattie, Positive Peer Influence has an effect size of 0.53. The level of thinking associated with an activity that requires participation goes beyond simple comprehension of text – it engages both the instigator and the audience. More importantly, participation helps fellow students learn from each other – and people tend to build their levels of self-efficacy depending on how those who are most close to them behave. In an article, *'Why We Should Embrace Mistakes in School'* (Eva, 2017), Amy Eva discusses the power of modelling, and in particular modelling self-compassion where she says, 'If we model and normalise the ups and downs of learning with our students, we can also share the power of self-compassion,' allow them to see that it is ok to not know the answer straight away and that mistakes happen, we shouldn't be too hard on ourselves. One area I know I sometimes struggle with (dare I admit it as an English teacher) is my spelling. There will be times when my mind goes blank when I am writing on the board, and I spell something incorrectly. When I was an newly qualified teacher (NQT), I hated this feeling – I thought about all those eyes on me, expecting me to be the expert, and here I was – mind blank – forgetting how to spell. I used to clam up, rub it out quickly and pretend I needed to check something on my computer, check the spelling then rush back hoping no one noticed. Now I embrace it, I tell my students I struggle, I get them to help me, I don't let them see any embarrassment, because I am not embarrassed – as I like to tell my students 'I may be awesome but unfortunately, I am not Superwoman!' I will ask them what I should do, how could I find the answer? Could they help me and tell me how to spell the word? They love this because they feel they have succeeded in being better than the teacher, but what I am really doing is modelling how to accept that sometimes we make mistakes. This is also the case when a student asks me a question that I don't know the answer to. It is so easy to fluff it and pretend that I know the answer, but what does that teach them? I will be honest, if I am not sure, I will say 'you know what, I don't know the answer to that – let's look it up,' and then we will research together. Again, this is modelling how to deal with a question you don't know the answer to – the best thing is to always be honest – something I do in interviews as well, if I am not sure of the answer, I will be honest and then attempt it the best that I can.

While Bandura focuses on the importance of observational learning and modelling, it is not just about watching each other, there is also a cognitive process taking place as well. Learners need to be able to internalise what they are seeing and understanding it to then mimic this behaviour. In an article *'Role models in career development: New directions for theory and research'* (Gibson, 2004) discusses the involvement of 'the psychological matching of cognitive skills and patterns of behaviour between a person and an observing individual.' This can then be broken down into four stages – attention, retention, reproduction, and motivation. Firstly, students need to actively see the behaviour they want to reproduce happen, they need to observe this behaviour taking place and how the role model handles the situation. If any of you have young children like me, you will know that they get to that age where they copy everything you do and say (sometimes to our horror), but they are watching how we respond to situations. Think about when you teach your children to say 'please' and 'thank you' – you model this behaviour as you do it, in shops, at the cafe, and in places where your children are paying attention and seeing this behaviour in play. Through repeated attention to this behaviour, they begin to internalise and retain what they have observed, you may hear them practise this behaviour with their teddies and toys, rehearsing the behaviour. The more they do this, the more likely they will be encouraged to use it when they have the opportunity to do so. I often hear my son in his room saying 'thank you, you're welcome' to his teddies before he goes to sleep. This means that when they are given the opportunity to showcase this skill in public, they feel more confident and are ready to try out their new skill, often followed by a 'good girl/boy' and a smile of positive reinforcement, which motivates them to do it again and again, and before you know it you have that polite child that always says 'please' and 'thank you.' Easy right? So, think about this when you are in your classroom – when you roll your eyes at an irritating comment, when you dismiss a student's question because it seems 'ridiculous,' or when you get annoyed when a student keeps asking the same question. Remember learning is visible, including facial expressions and actions. Model the behaviour you want your students to acquire – remember the good old saying, 'treat people the way you wish to be treated.'

Reading an article 'Modeling: Essential for Learning' (Lea, 2013), she discusses how modelling should become a deliberate part of our teaching and learning. When modelling she asks, do we:

1. Use visuals or examples that are relevant?
2. Model while thinking out loud so that students hear the process?

Self-efficacy – Developing staff and students

Key Concept	Lesson Objective: To be able to explain how meaning is being created.
P: Make a clear statement/point	It is clear at the start of this scene that the 2 girls have a close relationship.
E: Evidence from the Mise-en-scene to prove this	I know this because in the mise-en-scene the woman in the white coat has her arm around the other girl. Clearly this is a form of embrace showing she cares for the other girl, almost like she is hugging and reassuring her.
E: Evidence from the camera shots/movements used to prove this	
E. Evidence from the sound used to prove this	
E. Evidence from the editing used to prove this	
L. Link back to your point	

Figure 6.6 Paragraph modelling

3   Concisely communicate what we are doing and what is needed?
4   Present or model logically?
5   Present or model only what is needed and leave the extra 'stuff' out?

Modelling begins with the teacher doing the majority of the work, showing the process of how to be successful, this might be them completing one example. However, this leads to them slowly doing less and allowing students to take over (Figure 6.6).

Here I break down an answer for my students on how to write a successful answer, going through the steps one by one, explaining how I am developing my answer so they can see the process. I am also modelling my high expectations of what I would expect in their paragraphs so that they can see the level of detail I am going into. This is then shown on the next slide as a complete paragraph so that they can see what it would look like once all put together, also displaying the success criteria for them to remind them when they attempt their own paragraphs (Figure 6.7).

As this activity was done during Distance Learning, I used Microsoft OneNote for them to write their answers. For the less confident students, I then provided them with a structure

Key Concept

Lesson Objective: To be able to explain how meaning is being created.

It is clear at the start of this scene that the 2 girls have a close relationship. I know this because in the mise-en-scene the woman in the white coat has her arm around the other girl. Clearly this is a form of embrace showing she cares for the other girl, almost like she is hugging and reassuring her. The wide medium close up shot helps to emphasis this as we can see they are out in a field, clearly showing they have gone out somewhere together. The dialogue shows that the woman is giving advice by saying 'call them as you see them Bella' and the girl responds with a laugh and 'ok'. Clearly, they feel comfortable around each other. Then the non-diegetic soundtrack begins to play, which is upbeat which suggests they might be about to play a game. The editing is continuous here while the two women are speaking. This clearly shows they have a close relationship as they are comfortable around each other and embracing each other like family or friends.

SUCCESS CRITERIA:
- A point about what is happening in the scene has been made.
- It has been backed up with evidence (camera/sound/editing/mise-en-scene)
- It explains how/why meaning has been created.
- It links back to your main point.

Figure 6.7 Completed paragraph with success criteria

with sentence starters so that they are supported as they continue with their examples (Figure 6.8).

For the high achieving students, and as the other students get more confident, I can then begin to remove the support and allow students to use the original structure I provided with the success criteria to create their own paragraphs. This type of scaffolding helps students move through what Vygotsky called the 'Zone of Proximal Development' and the amount of support provided is gradually removed as they become more confident and competent at the task in hand (Stevens-Fulbrook, 2020).

Sharing best practices is another great way of showcasing and modelling to the students what is expected with a piece of work. I will often use WAGOLL (What A Good One Looks Like) on my Microsoft Team page to showcase when a student has done an excellent piece of work. What you could also do is use the Polly tool to get students to comment on why this would be considered a successful piece of work. This way of modelling does not just have to be for our students, but staff as well. In my school, we have Teaching and Learning Practitioners (TLPs), these are members of staff who have been selected due to their outstanding expertise in Teaching and Learning. It is the TLPs role to showcase and share their best practice to help other members of staff learn and gather new ideas. As part of this, I created the Teaching and Learning Gems

Self-efficacy – Developing staff and students

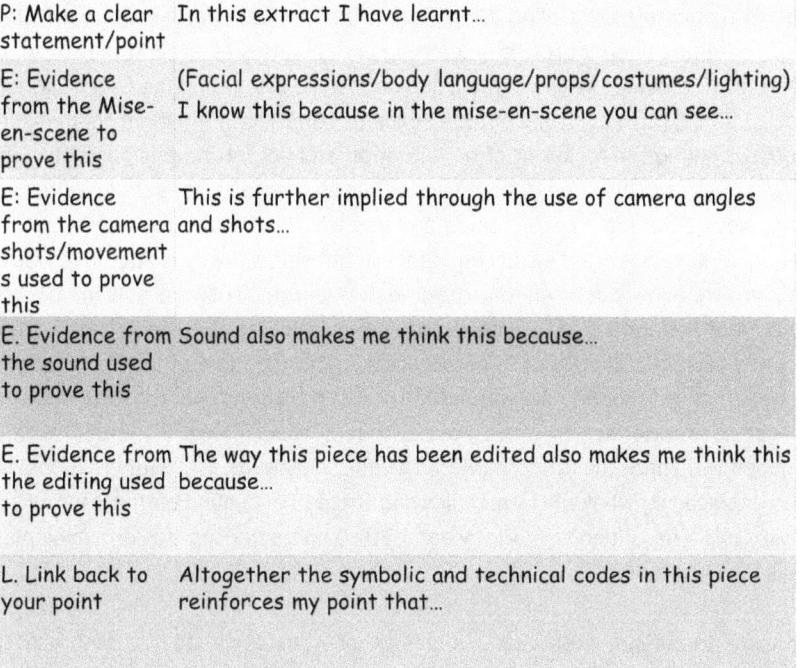

Figure 6.8 Sentence starter scaffolding

poster that was sent out to all staff at the beginning of each week, with a key focus and examples from our TLPs, linked to a shared folder where resources could be downloaded and used whenever necessary. I will go into more detail about this later in the Collective Efficacy chapter.

An important aspect that I think needs to be modelled for students, and teachers, is perseverance. With it being such an elusive concept, it is hard to physically show people such an important aspect of success. We all experience students in our class who would rather take the easier route of giving up before attempting a challenge – that 'I can't' mindset kicking in again. It is easy for them to sit silently and wait for you to check in on them, not attempting the work until you almost tell them the answer. This is where the power of 'yet' comes into play again, and those positive mindset strategies become so prevalent. As Joseph A. Pearson, MEd discusses in his article 'Mindsets Matter: The Power of Perseverance and Compassion' (2020), COVID-19 has led to an incredibly challenging couple of years, balancing all the different scenarios of teaching and learning in this new environment – teachers have had to embody problem-solving and perseverance to cope with the ever-changing climate. But what sets teachers apart is their mindsets, if they have a fixed mindset, they tend to struggle with change and adapting, but with a growth mindset, you are much more equipped with the resilience and perseverance to navigate through this new world of teaching and find the positives within. With a positive mindset, you become a much more effective facilitator, and you are more willing to seek new innovative ways to produce your lessons. I personally think there has been a massive rise in teachers sharing resources, with more discussions taking place online in Facebook groups. We were encouraged in our school to share resources and ideas with each other, trialling out different online apps that helped make our lessons engaging. There has been a growth in learning communities all around the world, I personally noticed it on LinkedIn where more educators were discussing ideas and vlogging their experiences. If nothing else, it gave me a sense of comradery, a feeling that we were all in this together, making the most out of the situation and not letting this pandemic beat us. In Angela Duckworth's (2019) book, 'Grit' she discusses the power of searching for ways that will change your situation – keep looking and you will find it, stop and you won't. When we begin to have that perseverance and confidence in our self-efficacy, we begin to lose that fear of failure, and we allow ourselves to experiment in lessons, trial out new ideas – that good old saying, 'if at first, you don't succeed, try again.' By doing this, we are also modelling to our peers and students the power of perseverance. Through doing this, when schools began to close again for a second lockdown, we were much more prepared, students were much more prepared, and we tackled it head on, confident in our new skills to deal with this new climate. When you share those successes with your colleagues, you begin to model your own WAGOLLs, showcasing what works and allowing them to also build on their self-efficacy too.

Chrissie, from The Undercover Classroom (2019) blogs her top tips on developing perseverance in the classroom:

1. 'Exposure' to difficult situations and challenges – she suggests five-minute brain teaser activities to get students thinking.
2. 'Attitude' – she teaches her students that things being hard is a good thing – it means their brains are growing. Make mistakes in front of the students and demonstrate your perseverance, making it a trait to be admired.
3. 'Patience' – remember you are embedding these traits into your students; it won't happen overnight. But be persistent and remain positive.
4. 'Acceptance' – understand that students develop at different speeds, accepting that some may take longer than others stops students feeling inferior because they are not there 'yet.'
5. 'Celebrate' success along the way.

Social and verbal persuasion

We all know that positive feeling we get when someone tells us we have done a good job – I know that I am one of those people that does need that positive reinforcement to truly believe in myself (a trait I am working on). Positive praise from our peers can have a significant effect on our self-belief, and I think that certain people can have much more influence on us. My husband always gives me positive praise and I, regrettably, don't always believe him – but when my peers give me praise, it feels much more justified and valuable, it is argued that the expertness and trustworthiness of the source have a significant impact on our self-efficacy (Eagly & Chaiken, 1993).

As teachers, we can be so critical of ourselves, but at the same time, we can also get so lost in our work that we don't think about others around us. Saying 'well done' or 'good job' can have a significant impact on a person's self-efficacy as well as their mental health, so I try to always remember this, and say well done whenever I see something good. Even more so with our students – they look up to their teachers and seek that reassurance that they are on the right track and are doing a good job. Receiving positive verbal feedback while doing complex tasks helps to persuade a person to believe in themselves. A person will grow in confidence much faster when encouraged regarding their ability to perform.

Verbal persuasion works at any age, but if you begin embedding this earlier on in a child's journey, they are more likely to build self-efficacy. When you don't give feedback, people take this to mean they are doing a good job – 'no feedback is good feedback' – but we know that this is not always the case. Without giving that verbal feedback to students, they could quite easily continue down the wrong path, in which case by the time they have finished, it is too late, which brings back that cycle of performance outcomes and mastering experiences. If a student is not supported sooner, they will either be confused as to whether they are doing what they need to do correctly, or they will not know what they need to do to fix any problems that have occurred and therefore see this as a failure on their behalf and therefore their self-efficacy will be lower. In order for feedback to work positively, feedback must be delivered both concisely and frequently. Both self-efficacy and performance are known to improve after receiving higher, more detailed levels of feedback (Beattie, Woodman, Fakehy, & Dempsey, 2015). I have already discussed different examples of verbal feedback earlier in the book, so I won't repeat myself here, but it is a good way of emphasising the importance of feedback. It serves not only to give students and staff constructive criticism but also develops their belief in themselves.

Tarosh Wangwongwiroj and Pratchayapong Yasri discuss in their correlation study between self-efficacy and growth mindset (2020) how verbal persuasion can positively affect self-efficacy provided it is given during action. When people are faced with challenges, verbal persuasion helps develop the feeling of accomplishment and capability, whereas when people are encouraged verbally but not specifically linked to a challenge, self-efficacy is not as likely to grow (Meyer, 1992). We have all had those students that instantly self-doubt – 'There is no point in me trying, I'll never be able to do it,' which leads to a lowered intellectual confidence. When I was working in a school in the UK, I came across so many students with such low self-esteem, that they felt they had been written off as failures. Many of these students came from broken homes and were not used to any form of positive praise, often resulting in attention-seeking and inappropriate behaviour. The first time I gave them the praise, they were embarrassed – they did not know what to do with this information. Up to this point, they had built a fixed mindset focusing on the negatives, building defences against those that criticised them because of their failure (Yeager, Trzesniewski, Tirri, Nokelainen, & Dweck, 2011). I will never forget one particular class, there were only seven in the class, the majority were low-ability boys, and a completely fixed mindset that they were at the bottom of the pile, with no motivation to try and succeed. They believed that they were unchangeable because they were born this way – such a sad mental state of mind to have. I remember when I began to build that relationship with them, and they started to feel comfortable enough with me to open up about their home lives – these students were desperate for a chance. One boy was the younger brother of a student that had been referred to a behaviour specialist unit a few years previously, and he was desperate to not end up like him but could feel himself slipping down that dark path. Blackwell et al (2007) conducted a study on children like this, who have a fixed mindset and saw many of them distrust putting in the effort, and again would fear failure, often leading to lower academic performance over time. As a class, they just needed that injection of positivity and verbal persuasion, in order to build up that self-efficacy. Mindsets can be developed, and ones that were once fixed can turn into growth mindsets, with the help of parents, peers, and teachers. In one of my schools, I introduced the idea of #ICan – reinforcing that positive language for learning.

Praise and verbal persuasion can build a belief system, but depending on the current mindset, different types of compliments can either develop or diminish how an individual views themselves. When you are praising, think about what type of praise you are giving – try not to praise the outcome, but the process students go through to get to the outcome, 'well done Hannah, you have been really resilient with that task, I know you found it hard at first, but you stuck with it,' or 'That was a fantastic example of independent enquiring there Zaahid, you didn't ask me for help, you did it by yourself, well done!' By praising the process, you are getting students to focus on their effort and skill development, rather than their intelligence, which could encourage the fixed mindset of either you can do it or you can't (Zentall & Morris, 2010). In a study undertaken in 2013, it was revealed that the use of process praise in younger children later developed into having a growth mindset in comparison to those that received task-based and ability praise led to a fixed mindset later in life. Regardless of whether they made a mistake or got the answer wrong, it is the fact that they have tried, and they have begun to use initiative to find the answer that is important. And again, this links back to the idea of perseverance and encouraging mistakes – so they got it wrong this time, they tried – that is what is important. As they learn the skills they used, they are able to reflect back and see where they went wrong and refine this – rather than having a lucky shot and not knowing how they got it right.

A part of Tarosh Wangwongwiroj and Pratchayapong Yasri research began with producing an online questionnaire for their high school students, both online and in school (due to COVID-19). This questionnaire had 18 statements in which students were asked to rate from 1 (strongly disagree) to 5 (strongly agree) (Table 6.1). These statements were divided into six categories – Growth Mindset (GM), Fixed Mindset (FM), Mastery Experience (ME), Vicarious Experience (VE), Verbal Persuasion on Intelligence (VP-I), and Verbal Persuasion on Effort (VP-E).

From their results, they were able to see that among the 206 students that took part in the questionnaire, there were more that had a growth mindset than those with a fixed mindset. It has been suggested that the higher the level of growth mindset, the better academic performance. Growth mindsets often lead to a willingness to take on challenges as they believe it will lead to self-betterment (Leroy, Bressoux, Sarrazin, & Trouilloud, 2007).

As I mentioned before, a way to help foster a growth mindset through verbal persuasion is making sure you are asking the right questions and giving the right feedback. I loved that class I taught in the UK, and by the end of that year, those boys made significant growth in their attainment – they finished that year believing #ICan.

Table 6.1 Self-efficacy and mindset questionnaire

Number:	Statement	Category Identified
1	I become confident in my ability when I complete a certain task.	ME
2	I become confident in my ability when other people tell me that I am good at what I am doing.	VP-I
3	I become confident in my ability when other people tell me to improve on something.	VP-E
4	I become confident in my ability when I see someone demonstrate a certain task beforehand.	VE
5	I accept others' feedback on areas to improve my own ability.	GM
6	I believe the reason why I am good at some skills is because of my natural ability.	FM
7	I become confident in my ability when I gain direct experience from a certain task.	ME
8	I become confident in my ability when other people give me compliments on my learning performance.	VP-I
9	I become confident in my ability when other people tell me that I can overcome challenges by working hard.	VP-E
10	I become confident in my ability when I see someone with a similar skillset as me accomplishing a certain task.	VE
11	I can manage to solve difficult problems if I try hard enough	GM
12	I believe that talents are something that is born with and cannot be developed.	FM
13	I become confident in my ability when I have a chance to do a certain task no matter what the results would be.	ME
14	I become confident in my ability when other people tell me that I am perfect.	VP-I
15	I become confident in my ability when other people tell me that I have done my best, even though the results are not desirable.	VP-E
16	I become confident in my ability when I see someone who has a similar level of competency as me doing a certain task.	VE
17	I believe that learning from mistakes is the path to success.	GM
18	I believe that the reason why I make mistakes is because of my own limited ability.	FM

Adapted from 'Self-Efficacy and Mindset Questionnaire' by Tarosh Wangwongwiroj, Pratchayapong Yasri is licensed under CC BY 4.0.

Emotional and physiological states

We all know our moods can have a massive impact on how we feel about tasks at hand. Our physical and emotional states can either motivate us forward or hold us back, and as a result, determine our likelihood of success or failure. Stress and anxiety will often lead to failure as we become unable to perform certain tasks (Pajares, 2002). In the blog post *'To Help Students Learn, Engage the Emotions'* (Lahey, 2016), Jessica discusses how research has been conducted into looking at how brain function changes when students are engaged emotionally, specifically in the regions that deal with cognition and memory. Over the years, I have come across so many different personal problems that affect our students – it doesn't matter if I am teaching in the UK or abroad, children all experience emotional and physiological issues, some more extreme than others. Some have external factors that play a huge role in their emotional state. Whatever the issue may be, there is strong research that shows a correlation between well-being and attainment: when well-being is low, so is a person's self-efficacy. I am not ashamed to admit that I suffer anxiety – have done since my teen years. When I have an anxiety attack, I cannot breathe, my heart races and I can't think straight. I usually have an attack after I have a new experience that may not have gone as well as I had hoped – leading to me having to go over and over the scenario in my head until I can make sense of the situation and begin thinking rationally again. In those moments, my self-esteem is completely low, but I have found my triggers, and learnt how to overcome these attacks – meaning my belief in my ability to get over these periods is strong, and therefore my self-efficacy is still high. We will always experience bad emotions – these are inevitable, but it is how we deal with them that matters, and with children, they need to learn how to deal with these emotions – especially teenagers with raging hormones!

When working with children, of any age, it is so important that we are paying attention to their well-being and emotional states, as this will impact our lessons with them. In order to foster positive outcomes, we need to be working with the child as a whole, even if we do only see them once or twice a week in some cases. Research has shown that education and health are closely linked and can contribute to a child's ability to benefit from our teaching and learning and reach their potential. As we discussed earlier in this chapter, success has a strong positive impact on how good they feel their lives are. Promoting physical and mental health in schools creates virtuous circles (Public Health England, 2014). The Ofsted 'School Inspection Handbook' (2021) specifically encourages 'developing pupils' confidence, resilience and knowledge so that they can keep themselves mentally healthy.'

During COVID-19, it became even more obvious that we needed to be checking in on our students and being alert to those that were choosing not to come online or access their lessons. Many of these children were locked down, in their homes, not being able to leave – after weeks of sitting in your bedroom, it is only a matter of time before the frustrations and depression kick in. We have students that have not set foot physically in a school building since March 2020 – they specifically are going to need support to reintegrate them back into physical school life.

Dr Martin Seligman originally defined well-being as having five pillars – PERMA (positive emotion, engagement, relationships, meaning, accomplishment) in his book, 'Flourish' (2012). This has since been developed by Margaret L. Kern, Lisbeth Benson, Elizabeth A. Steinberg, and Laurence Steinberg (n.d.) from the University of Pennsylvania and Temple University, to be suited for youths. As a result, they came up with the EPOCH:

- Engagement
- Perseverance
- Optimism
- Connectedness
- Happiness

By adapting it to make it more developmentally appropriate for younger students, it means we are focusing on adolescent well-being more accurately. One of our fantastic Heads of Year Graham Mallen introduced us to this at my current school, and it has been an invaluable source during COVID-19 as students are asked to complete it on a termly basis so that staff can monitor their well-being and their general moods and attitudes to learning. A copy of their EPOCH survey can be found on their website.

By thinking about these key areas collectively, it helps to ensure students are flourishing – when all five areas are high, it means students should be generally feeling good about themselves and working effectively (Huppert & So, 2013). Therefore, if they feel good in themselves, they are more likely to be active participants and feel more confident to explore new learning – having high self-efficacy. By checking in with students using the EPOCH, you can begin to form those strong relationships with your students and support them with their learning.

Mart Van Dinther et al (2011) studied the connection between self-efficacy and education and concluded that they both linked to a number of factors such as how students set goals for themselves academically. Those who had higher levels of self-efficacy tend to have healthy life habits which would lead to them doing better in school and being more organised.

As a post-16 tutor, I often see the stress increase in our students as they begin to apply to their universities. It is around this time that the realisation of how important their grades actually are starts to kick in. One of the ways we try to help encourage our students to cope with these challenges is by introducing them to Steve Oakes and Martin Griffin's VESPA programme (The VESPA Mindset, 2019). This acronym is broken down into five sections:

- **Vision**
- **Effort**
- **Systems**
- **Practice**
- **Attitude**

We start by discussing our students' vision with them – what is their goal moving forward? Some students begin post-16 with a very specific vision and have already mapped out exactly how they plan to get there – which refers back to Duckworth's idea of 'Grit,' but many students have no idea what it is they want to do with the rest of their lives – I for sure had no idea. If you asked me what I wanted to do with my life when I was 17, I would say I wanted to be 'in the media' – whatever that actually meant. I had no idea what part of 'the media' I was interested in, I just knew I loved the subject, and I was good at it. But then again, I loved history and English Literature, so I chose those subjects too.

A Harvard Business Study looked into the relation of goal setting and success and found out that 83% of people do not have any goals, 14% have a plan in mind but have never written down their goals, and only 3% have written goals. The 14% who at least have a plan are 10 times more successful than those with no goals, and the 3% with their goals written down are 3x more successful than the 14% (Faircloth, 2019). When students have a clear vision of where they want to go and what they want to do, their belief in being able to succeed is much higher and therefore their self-efficacy is higher. But it is ok not to know the big picture at 17, so we start small. Asking 'what is your goal' is not the best way of unlocking a vision, because how are you supposed to answer that when you are not entirely sure? This just leads to frustration and embarrassment, especially if others around you are so clear and proud of their goal, with a clear pathway already mapped out. Instead, we start with ten questions that Oaks and Griffin created, allowing them to reflect on their current situation, and try to figure out what it is they might like to do. Some of these questions are:

- If you could only take one subject, what would it be and why?
- What do you do in your spare time?
- What job would you do for free?
- What puts a smile on your face?

We also discuss different types of goals – Push and Pull goals. The former being goals set by other people around them such as their target grades or their parents pushing them into a certain career. These types of goals remove the ownership from the students, and therefore they lack the motivation to strive for them. Whereas pull goals come from the passions and desires of the students – which will often lead to higher attendance, effort, and grades.

Through these one to one discussions with students, you can begin to establish what it is that sparks their enthusiasm – this usually leads to what it is they would like to pursue at university and as a career later on. So, the next focus is on their Effort – what does this actually mean to students? Most of the time, when you say 'you're not putting in enough effort' it is usually because they don't know what that actually looks like. They will base their efforts on the people they surround themselves with. If they see a student in their friendship group doing next to no work, they will automatically think they are putting more effort in than that person – that doesn't mean they are putting in enough effort though. We all know A-Levels is a huge step up from GCSEs and this often comes as a bit of a shock to students, so we used the VESPA 3Rs to help show that effort is like a habit – something that needs to be built into their day-to-day routine. These are:

1. Reminder – create a trigger that will remind you that it is now time to study. This might be getting a drink ready to sit down to work or setting an alarm.
2. Routine: turn this reminder into part of your daily routine so that you can complete the action of studying. When your alarm goes off, you know that this is the time to remove distractions and begin working. Another great author that provides useful ways of building habits is B. J. Fogg in his book 'Tiny Habits' (2020)
3. Reward – you should feel proud of yourself for completing the task at hand, give yourself some credit, and praise your achievements. This could be a little chocolate bar or allowing yourself to watch one of your favourite TV shows.

When I was at university, I was the queen of procrastination – I thought just sitting in the library was enough to show my dedication – however, staring at a screen or not turning a page in my book for an hour probably wasn't the most effective use of my time. So, I began to find ways to keep myself motivated – I created a routine of getting up at 9 am and walking to the library after my breakfast. I would stop off at the co-op on the way and buy myself a sharing bag of Minstrels, I then would place the treat at the end of a chapter and allow myself to eat it once I was completed. Probably not a great idea for my waist, or for the library book – but it worked for me.

So, once a vision has been established and students are clearer on how to improve the effort they are putting into their studies, to ultimately achieve that goal, we then begin to discuss the Systems that can be put into place in order to help them succeed. Again, this links to resilience and perseverance because not every system works for every student – finding the right one might take time. From my own past experience, low-system students are usually the ones that are characterised as being consistently late, bad organisation, lack of sleep, and high stress levels (I am sure we can all picture a student that matches this description!). These students in particular need the support of systems. Some examples of these are given in Figure 6.9.

Once they have completed their lesson, students are all of a sudden faced with study periods – something we constantly stress to our students is not the time to be catching up with Love Island or the X-Factor. So, once they come out of class and settle themselves down in the Common Room or the Library – how do they then manage their time and study needs? Again, we have to build up that self-efficacy belief that they have the tools they need to succeed. They may choose to sit and stare at their textbook for an hour and procrastinate (we've all been there), but at least they have the tools should they choose to use them. When they have multiple projects all due around the same time, they need to have the tools to manage and prioritise. We would all like to focus on the topic/job we like the most or are the best at, but that usually means we leave the bits we don't like until the end, which often leads to more stress and worry and ultimately failure in that task. Getting students to plot their subjects on a graph like this will help them prioritise which piece of

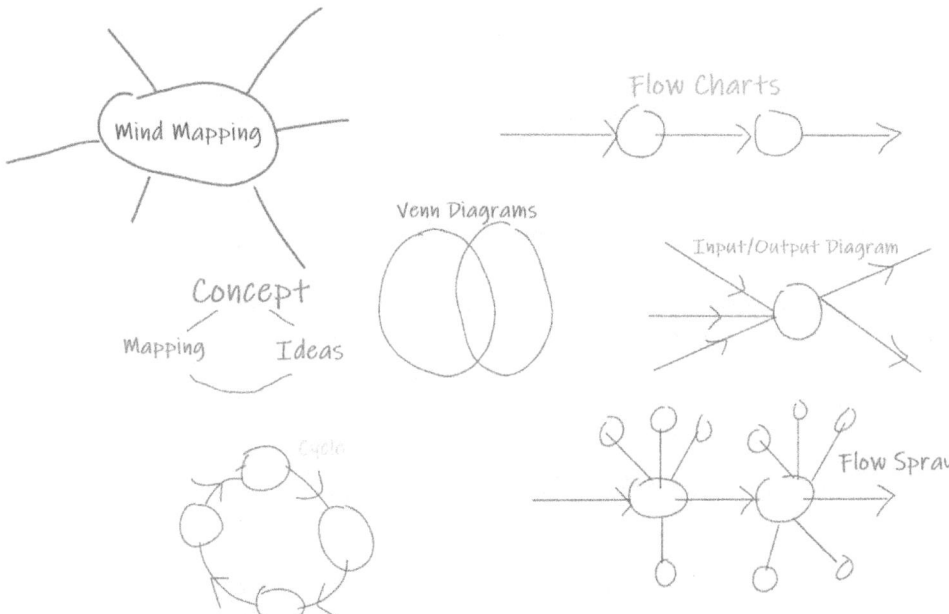

Figure 6.9 Examples of systems for students

98 *Self-efficacy – Developing staff and students*

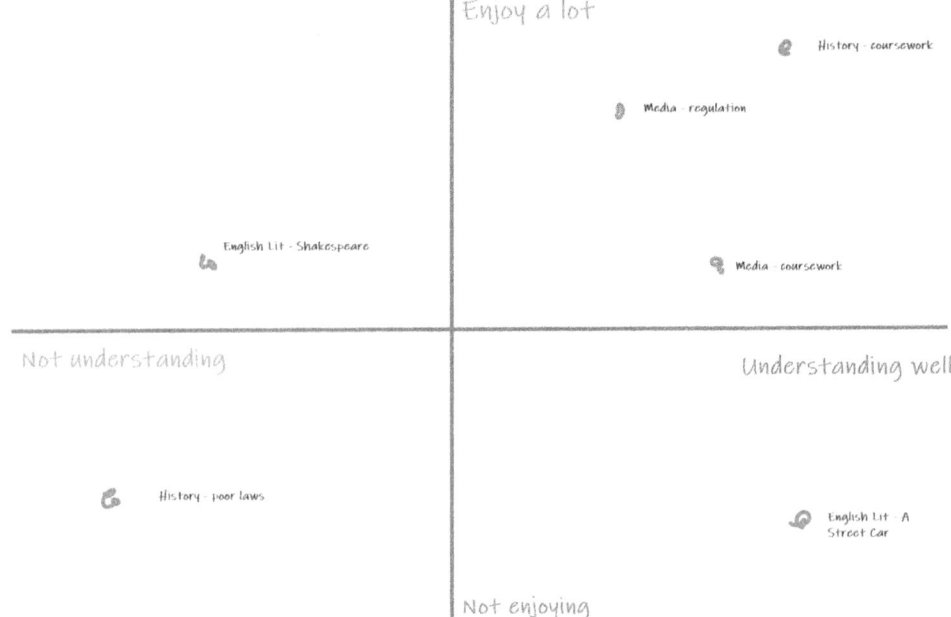

Figure 6.10 Organisation task for students

work needs more focus and attention – it also allows them to see if there are any areas that they need more support in and need more clarification on (Figure 6.10).

Once systems have been put into place, the next part is practice – consolidating the learning. Revision techniques are really useful here, providing students with examples of how to take their learning further and apply it to a range of examples. Here Oakes and Griffin (2021) give a great worksheet in their A Level VESPA Mindset Workbook, that gets students thinking about what type of revision they tend to do – often when you ask them, they are unsure what exactly is 'revision' or how to do it successfully. This activity gets them to look at a range of revision examples but also determine which will help them with the learning of content, which will help develop skills and which will provide them with feedback (Figure 6.11).

By embedding self-regulation into the day-to-day tasks for students, they are able to grow their self-efficacy, as they become more confident with using their time effectively. You can contact Steve Oakes and Martin Griffin on Twitter – @VESPAMindset to discuss their ideas and worksheets more. I have to say Steve was, hands down, one of the best speakers I have ever listened to.

You can always measure self-efficacy in your class or school using the general self-efficacy scale (GSE) which was developed by Ralf Schwarzer and Matthias Jerusalem (1995). This is composed of 8 statements in which students rate on a scale of 1 (strongly disagree) to 5 (strongly agree) (Table 6.2).

Calculating the score by taking the average grade across all eight responses will determine how strong your students' self-efficacy is – the higher one's score is, the stronger their self-efficacy is.

What sort of revision activities do you do? Tick either always, sometimes or never next to each statement.

	Sometimes	Always	Never
Reading through class notes (c)			
Using resources on online (c)			
Using course textbooks (c)			
Using mind maps diagrams (c)			
Making / re-making class notes (c)			
Highlighting or colour coding (c)			
Flash cards (c)			
Using a revision wall to display learning (c)			
Writing exam answers under timed conditions (s)			
Reading model answers (s)			
Using past exam questions to plan out answers (s)			
Marking your own work to a mark scheme (s)			
Studying mark schemes or examiner's reports (f)			
Working with other students in groups/pairs (f)			
Comparing model answers against your own work (f)			
Creating your own exam questions (f)			
Handing in extra exam work for marking (f)			
One to one discussion with teachers / tutors (f)			

Did you notice the categories next to each item?

c = content
s = skills
f = feedback

Put in your scores for each category here:
c =
s =
f =

Figure 6.11 Revision questionnaire for students

Adapted from: Oakes and Griffin (2019).

Table 6.2 General self-efficacy scale

	Statement	1	2	3	4	5
1	I believe that I am capable of achieving most of the goals that I set myself.					
2	I am certain that I will accomplish difficult tasks that I face.					
3	Overall, I am capable of obtaining outcomes that I think are important to me.					
4	I believe I can succeed at most things I put my mind to.					
5	I can overcome many challenges successfully.					
6	I can perform effectively on many different tasks confidently.					
7	I do most tasks well in comparison to other people.					
8	I perform well even if when it is tough.					

Adapted from the General Self-Efficacy Scale by Schwarzer and Jerusalem (1995).

100 *Self-efficacy – Developing staff and students*

So, as you have just read, there are a range of ways of understanding and improving self-efficacy – developing that belief in one's ability and embedding perseverance and resilience. By actively doing these things on a daily basis, you will be able to see those positive changes in both yourself and your students – the power of 'yet' couldn't be more prevalent here. Stick with it, consistency is key.

> **Chapter Summary**
>
> - Self-efficacy is the belief in one's ability to overcome certain tasks and challenges.
> - Bandura broke down self-efficacy into four sections.
> - Mastery and experience – allowing students to develop perseverance by making mistakes. Giving them opportunities to be successful to encourage them to continue to actively participate in tasks.
> - Vicarious experiences and social models – being able to model for students to allow them to see how to be successful, then encourage them to try themselves. Modelling is important, not just for a specific task, but how to deal with certain situations as well.
> - Verbal persuasion – providing students and staff with verbal feedback that will encourage a growth mindset and encourage them to be motivated to continue with challenges, no matter how hard they are perceived to be.
> - Emotional and psychological states – working with students to provide them with tools to help with their well-being and managing the stresses of schools. Using the EPOCH to measure well-being can help to provide students with specific support.
> - You can use the GSE to measure the self-efficacy of your students.
>
> **So, what does an 'outstanding' teacher do?**
>
> Develops their student's self-efficacy by building up their resilience and empowering them with the positive term 'yet.' Creating a safe space where it is ok to make mistakes – encouraging perseverance through effective modelling.

References

Bandura, A. (1977). *Social Learning Theory*. New York: General Learning Press.
Bandura, A. (1997). *Self-efficacy: The exercise of control*. New York: Freeman.
Beattie, S., Woodman, T., Fakehy, M., & Dempsey, C. (2016). The role of performance feedback on the self-efficacy-performance relationship. *Sport, Exercise, and Performance Psychology*, 5(1), 1-13.
Blackwell, L. S., Trzesniewski, K. H., & Dweck, C. S. (2007). Implicit theories of intelligence predict achievement across an adolescent transition: A longitudinal study and an intervention. *Child Development*, 78(1), 246-263. https://doi.org/10.1111/j.1467-8624.2007.00995.x
Covington, M. V. (1999). *The will to learn a guide for motivating young people*. Cambridge: Cambridge University Press.
Dinther, M. V., Dochy, F., & Segers, M. S. (2011). Factors affecting students' self-efficacy in higher education. *Educational Research Review*, 6, 95-108.

Duckworth, A. (2019). *GRIT: The power of passion and perseverance young readers edition*. New York; London: Simon & Schuster Books.
Dweck, C. S. (2017). *Mindset: Changing the way you think to fulfil your potential*. London: Robinson.
Eagly, A. H., & Chaiken, S. (1993). *The psychology of attitudes*. Belmont, CA: Wadsworth Cengage Learning.
Eva, A. (2017, November 28). *Why we should embrace mistakes in school*. Retrieved from Greater Good website. https://greatergood.berkeley.edu/article/item/why_we_should_embrace_mistakes_in_school
Faircloth, E. (2019, September 19). *Those with goals are 10× more likely to succeed* [Blog]. Retrieved from Biggerpockets.com website. https://www.biggerpockets.com/blog/2015-11-06-set-goals-for-2016
Fogg, B. J. (2020). *Tiny Habits: The small changes that change everything*. New York.: Houghton Mifflin Harcourt Publishing Company.
Gibson, D. E. (2004). Role models in career development: New directions for theory and research. *Journal of Vocational Behavior*, 65(1), 134–156. https://doi.org/10.1016/s0001-8791(03)00051-4
Hook, P., & Mills, J. (2011). *SOLO taxonomy: A guide for schools. Book 1, a common language for learning*. Laughton: Essential Resources.
Huppert, F. A., & So, T. T. C. (2013). Flourishing across Europe: Application of a new conceptual framework for defining well-being. *Social Indicators Research*, 110, 837–861. http://dx.doi.org/10.1007/s11205-011-9966-7
Kapur, M. (2008). Productive failure. *Cognition and Instruction*, 26(3), 379–425.
Kegan, R., & Lahey, L. (2001, November 10). *The real reason people won't change*. Retrieved from Harvard Business Review website. https://hbr.org/2001/11/the-real-reason-people-wont-change
Kern, M., Benson, L., Steinberg, E., & Steinberg, L. (n.d.). *The EPOCH measure of adolescent well-being*. https://www.peggykern.org/uploads/5/6/6/7/56678211/epoch_measure_of_adolescent_well-being_102014.pdf
Lahey, J. (2016, May 4). *To help students learn, engage the emotions*. Retrieved from Well website. https://archive.nytimes.com/well.blogs.nytimes.com/2016/05/04/to-help-students-learn-engage-the-emotions/
Lazarus, R. S., & Launier, R. (1978). Stress-related transactions between person and environment. In L. A. Pervin, & M. Lewis (Eds.), *Perspectives in interactional psychology* (pp. 287–327). Boston, MA: Springer.
Lea, K. (2013, March 20). *Modeling: Essential for learning*. Retrieved from Edutopia website. https://www.edutopia.org/blog/modeling-essential-for-learning-karen-lea
Leroy, N., Bressoux, P., Sarrazin, P., & Trouilloud, D. (2007). Impact of teachers' implicit theories and perceived pressures on the establishment of an autonomy supportive climate. *European Journal of Psychology of Education*, 22(4), 529–545. https://doi.org/10.1007/bf03173470
Meyer, W. (1992). Paradoxical effects of praise and blame on perceived ability. In W. Stroebe, & M. Hewstone (Eds.), *European review of social psychology* (Vol. 3, pp. 259–83). Chichester: Wiley.
Nottingham, J. (2017). *The learning challenge: How to guide your students through the learning pit to achieve deeper understanding*. Thousand Oaks, CA: Corwin, A Sage Company.
Oakes, S., & Griffin, M. (2019). *The VESPA mindset workbook: 40 activities for FE students that transform commitment, motivation and productivity*. London: Crown House Publishing.
Oakes, S., & Griffin, M. (2021). *The VESPA mindset workbook: 4 revised edition. 40 activities for transforming student commitment, motivation and productivity*. London: Crown House Publishing.
Ofsted. (2021). *School inspection handbook*. Retrieved from GOV.UK website. https://www.gov.uk/government/publications/school-inspection-handbook-eif/school-inspection-handbook
Pajares, F. (2002). *Overview of social cognitive theory and of self-efficacy*. Retrieved July 17 2021, from Uky.edu website: https://www.uky.edu/~eushe2/Pajares/eff.html
Pearson, J. A. (2020, August 21). *Mindsets matter: The power of perseverance and compassion*. Retrieved from Moreland University website. https://moreland.edu/resources/blog-insights/jnpr7rca24kr9ekg7pmq3avl7vhjj9
Public Health England. (2014). *The link between pupil health and wellbeing and attainment: A briefing for head teachers, governors and staff in education settings*. https://assets.publishing.service.gov.uk/government/uploads/system/uploads/attachment_data/file/370686/HT_briefing_layoutvFINALvii.pdf
Schwarzer, R., & Jerusalem, M. (1995). Generalized self-efficacy scale. Measures in health psychology: A user's portfolio. *Causal and Control Beliefs*, 1(1), 35–37.
Seligman, M. E. P. (2012). *Flourish: A visionary new understanding of happiness and well-being*. New York: Atria Publishing Group.
Stevens-Fulbrook, P. (2020). *Vygotsky, Piaget and Bloom: The definitive guide to their educational theories with examples of how they can be applied*. Self-published: Paul Stevens-Fulbrook.

Undercoverclassroom. (2019, June 25). *Teaching perseverance to students – Undercover classroom*. Retrieved from https://www.undercoverclassroom.com/teaching-perseverance-to-students/

Wangwongwiroj, T., & Yasri, P. (2020). A correlational study of self-efficacy and mindset: Building growth mindset through mastery experience and effort-based verbal persuasion. *Psychology and Education, 58*(2), 5260–5268.

Yeager, D. S., Trzesniewski, K. H., Tirri, K., Nokelainen, P., & Dweck, C. S. (2011). Adolescents' implicit theories predict desire for vengeance after peer conflicts: Correlational and experimental evidence. *Developmental Psychology, 47*(4), 1090–1107. https://doi.org/10.1037/a0023769

Zakrzewski, V. (2013, December 5). *How to help kids overcome fear of failure*. Retrieved from Greater Good website: https://greatergood.berkeley.edu/article/item/how_to_help_kids_overcome_fear_of_failure#thank-influence

Zentall, S. R., & Morris, B. J. (2010). 'Good job, you're so smart': The effects of inconsistency of praise type on young children's motivation. *Journal of Experimental Child Psychology, 107*(2), 155–163. https://doi.org/10.1016/j.jecp.2010.04.015

7 Collective teacher efficacy

Now we have established what self-efficacy is, it is time to move on to 'Collective Teacher Efficacy.' I am a big fan of CTE, and it is something I often #hashtag when I am on LinkedIn or Twitter – the power of working as a collective, using your experts to ensure Teaching and Learning thrives is phenomenal, something that Hattie has in fact rated as having one of the biggest effect sizes. We looked at the power that belief in oneself can have, just imagine how much that power grows when a collective is all working towards that same belief. With a collective focus and belief, it becomes more significant and impactful than any other factor related to student achievement – including their socioeconomic background, double the effect of their prior learning, and triples the effect of home environment (Donohoo, 2017).

Just like self-efficacy, CTE builds on the four key areas set out by Bandura – mastering experiences, social role models, social and verbal persuasion, and emotional and physiological states. If you can build on these four areas for yourself, then you can begin to work on these as a collective. CTE is a little like a house of cards – take one away and it can all come crashing down. It really is a team effort building on those positive attributes to strengthen your team and develop you all collectively.

Our role as teachers is to educate – the sole purpose we got into teaching. For the majority of our careers, we are just one teacher in a classroom of potentially 30 students – all watching us and, hopefully, learning from us. If you are an excellent teacher, your students are going to thrive, and you will continue year on year to succeed in helping them achieve or exceed their targets – that is all of our aims. However, there are teachers that do struggle in the classroom, be it with behaviour management, teaching strategies, or building relationships, which could ultimately lead to students floundering. Have you ever sat in the staff room discussing a particular student you are struggling with, and that smug teacher says, 'Oh he is wonderful for me, I never have an issue'? This can be really demoralising as you begin to question what it is that you might be doing wrong. While we will often talk to other teachers and maybe even be brave enough to ask for help or support, for the most part, our jobs can be very lonely – if we have a particularly busy day, we could go the whole day without actually interacting with another adult. While people like to think they know what life as a teacher is like – they don't! It is tiring, stressful, and sometimes never-ending. You can easily end the week feeling flat and dejected as you question your efficacy and wonder, 'am I even having an impact?'

Table 7.1 Effect sizes of influences on student attainment

Influence	Effect Size
Collective teacher efficacy	1.57
Teacher clarity	0.75
Feedback	0.75
Teacher-student relationships	0.72
Prior achievement	0.65
Socioeconomic status	0.52
Home environment	0.52
Parental involvement	0.49
Concentration/persistence/engagement	0.48

Adapted from Hattie (2012).

CTE is when teachers, collectively, align their vision and work together to ensure teaching and learning is developed with a shared idea of the outcome. We should all believe in our ability to reach *every* single student we work with, even those tough, unmotivated students, and work together as a collective to ensure this is happening. When this is happening, as mentioned earlier, this has a much bigger effect size than the other factors that potentially affect student achievement as can be seen in Table 7.1.

What is so great about CTE is the coming together of those who are in the classroom every single day, sharing experiences together to help improve those challenges within the classroom. It is not SLT telling you what you should do, it is not outside agents giving you an idea for you to trial – it is working with your team and utilising your experts so that high standards are being enforced in every classroom. We all got into this profession because we want our students to succeed, whether it was Dangerous Minds, Dead Poets Society, or Mona Lisa Smile that encouraged us, we all wanted to be part of that pivotal moment in a student's life when the penny finally drops. Whether you are in a Secondary department team or a Primary year group team, you ALL want your students to have the best education possible and we are all responsible for each student we teach, regardless of what we are teaching them (Eells, 2011). It is about discussing with your team what your outcome goal is, how are you collectively going to achieve it? Can everyone in the team get the same results? If not, how can you change this so that all students are equally getting the best education? Am I having the same impact in my lesson as Mrs Brown in another lesson? How can we ensure we are all challenging our students to the same extent? This isn't about teachers being better than the rest – it's about finding out the strengths of the departments and collaborating together to help 'lift' all teachers; 'use the powers of collective wisdom to ensure all teachers are achieving agreed magnitudes of effect on student learning' (Hattie, 2015, p. 25).

The first part of encouraging CTE is down to mind frames – just like students, teachers also need to adopt a growth mindset in order to be truly reflective of their practice and agree and accept that there will be some teachers that are just more effective in some aspects of their careers than others. I know what my strengths are in the classroom, but I also know I have areas that need developing – being Outstanding doesn't mean being the best at everything, it means being reflective and accepting support – regardless of how many years you have been teaching. For those of you just starting out in the profession, my advice to you is never to think you have finished learning – you haven't! Keep a growth mindset and continue to develop professionally – even when you've been teaching for 10, 20, or 30 years – keep reading and researching! Those of you who have been teaching a while, you guys have amazing expertise – share! You have a lot to give to the profession for people to learn from! But do not think that means you are above continuing your own learning – read an educational journal, discuss this with your team – you may be surprised in what you learn (by you reading this book right now means you are on the right track, even if you don't agree with me!). One of the major things that hold teaching and learning back are the teachers that maintain a fixed mindset – often those that have been teaching a while and have got themselves into a routine. Why should they change, they have been doing it this way for years and it works fine for them?! But my question is – is fine good enough? Did we get in this profession just to be a 'fine' teacher, or did we get in this profession to provide students with the best opportunities? Another argument I often hear is 'we don't have time to change and trial out new ideas – we will just stick with what we know works' – but is it working? Ok, so you prepare your students for the exams they must sit now, but what about their futures? Are you preparing them for the world beyond school? Are you developing their skills and self-efficacy? Working collaboratively helps you see different approaches and can change you from being a 'fine' teacher to being a 'great' teacher. Let's stop isolating ourselves in our classrooms and instead work collaboratively to improve our effectiveness. While CTE has such strong research behind why it is such a successful approach to student achievement, it can also have a negative effect when staff do not share the same collective vision and belief – if you are not willing to adapt and be a change agent, then CTE will have the opposite effect – which is much more detrimental to student achievement (Donohoo, 2017). Kanter (2006) argued that the absence of efficacy are key reasons why organisations tend to fail. As I mentioned in the chapter before, setting goals makes you more likely to achieve, 'teachers with high sense of efficacy are more willing to take responsibility for student successes and failures than teachers who score low on teaching efficacy measures' (Georgiou, Christou, Stavrinides, & Panaoura, 2002, p. 585).

Hattie and Zierer introduced the *10 mindframes for visible learning* (2017), and one of them that is relevant here is 'I Collaborate' – we get students to work in teams all the time, and group work is a regular strategy to help them learn, so why don't we do it more? We tell our students the benefits of working in a team:

- Gives opportunities to explore more ideas
- Provides diverse perspectives
- Shares workload
- Develops confidence
- Encourages more discussions

There are lots more benefits, but as you can see when we ask our students to do teamwork, we are providing them with so many opportunities – why would we not want to do this ourselves? I actually think COVID-19 has helped us in this aspect – we were all thrown into the deep end, all around the world. This wasn't just one country or one small area, it was a worldwide pandemic! For the first time ever, I was sharing information and starting conversations with people all around the world. We were all sharing our experiences and methods of online learning – we were a community working together to make sure learning continued at no cost. 'This crisis has created an unprecedented context that has brought to the fore teacher leadership, creativity and innovation … teachers have worked individually and collectively to find solutions and create new learning environments for their students to ensure that learning never stops' (UNESCO, 2020).

Let us explore some of the things we can do with our teams to encourage more CTE. In Hattie's book, he asks you to think about these short reflection questions:

I am very good at …

- *saving time by sharing work with other teachers.*
- *sharing responsibility in a team.*

I know perfectly well …

- *that failures can be overcome in a team.*
- *that responsibility can be shared in a team.*

My goal is always to …

- *consolidate strengths through teamwork.*
- *overcome failures in my team.*

I am thoroughly convinced …

- *that strengths can be consolidated in a team.*
- *that it is important to cooperate with my colleagues.*

While teachers can be successful on their own, delivering outstanding lessons and forming fantastic relationships with students, 'they can be even more successful if they work together with others' (Hattie & Zierer, 2018, p. 57). Hattie also states nine steps towards developing collective efficacy within an organisation (Table 7.2).

When we first started our visible learning journey, I created a weekly poster that I shared with staff called the 'Teaching and Learning Gems.' The purpose of this was to initially get staff sharing best practices, where we had a shared resource folder that all members of staff had access to. Each week there would be a specific theme, such as starters, plenaries, SOLO activities, etc., and I would ask staff to upload any resources they used into the shared folder during the week (Figure 7.1). I would then showcase these on the following poster to encourage staff to try them out in their lessons.

Although Hattie discusses that CTE is not just about sharing resources, this was a good way of building that initial community with our staff – getting them involved in a collective approach of sharing best practice. But what Hattie is focused on is deeper than this – it is about how when 'teachers collectively think about their impact and student progress is most relevant to the success for their students' (Hattie & Zierer, 2018, p. 58).

Table 7.2 Nine steps to developing collective efficacy

1	I understand that 'I cause learning.'
2	I understand the importance of high expectations for all students and agree that 'we are jointly responsible for each student.'
3	Evaluative thinking relates to seeking to evaluate the impact of my teaching.
4	Having the 'I' skills (I am self-aware, I am a learner about my impact, I can manage conflict and queries about my impact) and the 'we' skills (I have high levels of social sensitivity, I wish to have a shared purpose to improve, I am prepared to problem solve, I trust and respect the views of others).
5	I work with others to seek evidence of impact to feed and justify our high levels of confidence to make the difference that matters.
6	I can work with others to agree on the sufficient and high levels of growth we aim to achieve over this school year.
7	I am prepared to focus on excellent diagnosis of what the students bring to the class, how they undertake their learning, and the impact I have on these students.
8	I work and evaluate together with my colleagues to have a common conception of progress and a joy in the high positive impact we are having, and to continue to work together on maximizing this impact.
9	The role of school leaders to legitimate, support, esteem, and create the trust and time needed to develop collective efficacy.

Source: Adapted from Hattie and Zierer (2018).

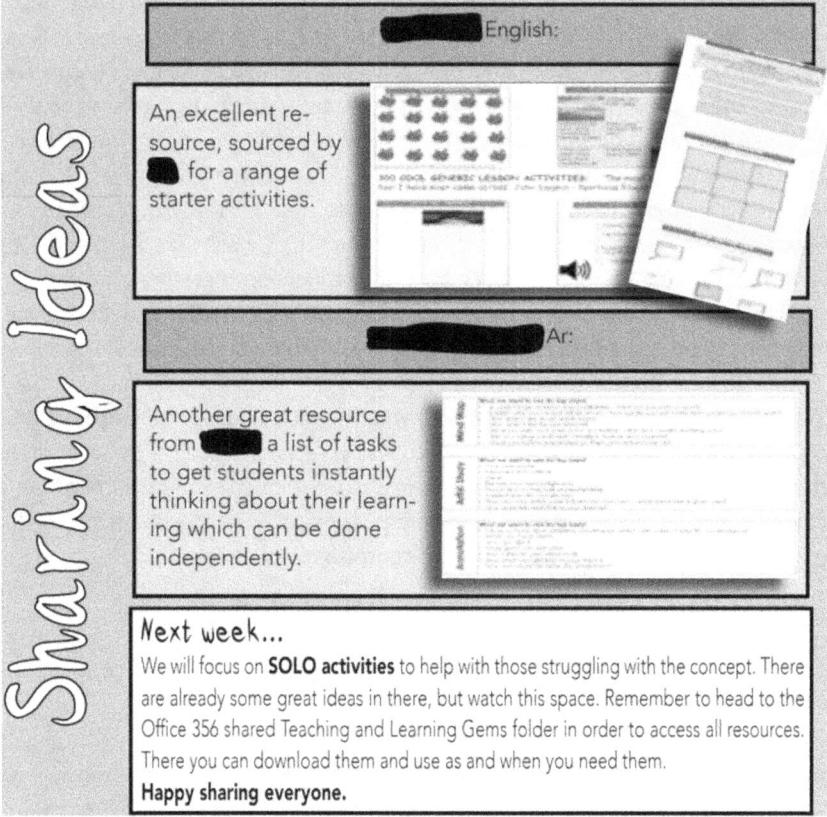

Figure 7.1 Example from the teaching and learning GEM poster

Collective language for learning

Have you ever taught a class and think they are not really paying much attention to you, but when you come to mark their work you realise they have almost directly quoted you? Sometimes, without realising it, we often drill in certain words and phrases when we are teaching a topic, and these are retained by our students – and while they might not use them in the most appropriate or accurate way, they do attempt to use them. When I was teaching my top set Year 11 English Language class, I tried to drill in evaluative verbs so that they began to use them more in their writing – I have never seen the word 'bolster' used as much as that class did. I didn't know whether to be proud of their growing vocabulary or disappointed that that was the only verb they seemed to stick with! But this just shows you the power words and language can have, especially when they are repeated. Think retrieval practice – the more you enforce a word/phrase/idea, revisiting it every lesson, the stronger the impact and more likely it is going to move from short-term memory to long-term memory. I still remember 'asseyez-vous' – probably the only French that has stuck with me since my school days, but it was said at the start of every lesson, and I have retained it. Therefore, it is important to establish a common language for learning that you as a school want to focus on. What are the keywords or phrases you want your students to be able to recall and understand, regardless of what lesson they are in? These could be learner characteristics, dispositions, or core values that you want to make explicit to your students so that they can understand how learning is taking place. After collectively discussing our vision for what we wanted our students to be able to achieve in Secondary, we came up with three learner attributes – Passive, Resilient, and Motivated Learners.

In order to come up with these different types of learner attributes, we started by holding a whole school (primary and secondary) CPD session in which we asked staff to discuss and write down their ideas of 'what a good learner looks like.' Hargreaves and Fullan (2012) really value the importance of giving teachers the power to be a part of big decisions, by allowing our staff to be involved in this process and hearing their voices, we were entrusting and empowering them to be the driving force behind change, and therefore increasing our collective efficacy and staff buy-in. 'Everyone, regardless of what position is held, has the ability to create change and possesses leadership qualities that can be cultivated' (Donohoo, 2017, p. 28). From this information, myself and two of my colleagues, Callum Neale and Samantha Pyper, worked on creating a visual pathway of what these would look like through KS2-KS5.

Due to the collective approach of all staff, we were able to come to an agreed vision of what our best learners would look like – we set our high standards through an agreed approach, using the voices of those that spend every day in the classroom with these students. For our Secondary School, these attributes became defined as:

Am I a motivated learner? When I learn I

- Take full responsibility for my own progress.
- Always seek challenge and support when I need it.
- I love solving problems in lessons – I see it as a challenge.
- I always try hard to accomplish the goals I set for myself through self-direction.
- I am proactive, and I look for ways to broaden my own knowledge.

- I always participate in lessons.
- I seek excellence, I am not frightened or put off by failure – I see it as a chance to 'do better' and learn from my mistakes.
- I embody the core values of the academy to the fullest.

Am I a resilient learner? When I learn I

- frequently complete tasks fully and to the best of my ability in lessons.
- frequently take responsibility for my own learning.
- I take the initiative to actively review and improve my work before asking my teachers.
- frequently undertake extension activities.
- produce homework to a very high standard.
- I am conscious of my attainment, and I am mostly driven more by my grade than by the progress I make.
- I am very keen to do well.
- frequently display the core values of the academy.

Am I a passive learner? When I learn I

- mostly rely on my teachers to make progress in lessons.
- complete my classwork, but it's not always to the best of my ability.
- set goals for myself and struggle to achieve them.
- am not in the habit of reviewing or reflecting on my own work.
- prefer not to participate in lesson discussions and activities.
- sometimes embody the core values of the academy, but mainly in subjects, I enjoy.

These attributes are now displayed on every classroom wall, as well as stuck into the front of students' books. We also encourage teachers to refer to these throughout the lesson so that students can reflect on what type of learner they are being and can remind themselves of what attributes they need to have in order to improve. Likewise, we use these attributes as part of our reporting, so we can tell parents which of these attributes their child is currently achieving.

Similarly, our Primary school also came up with their own language for learning, using memorable alliterative phrases with images for the younger students. Again, the primary teachers collectively agreed on the key skills they believed should be reinforced with our students. As you can see below, these have become eye-catching logos for our younger students, designed by a very talented primary school teacher, Lynn Kolesky (Figures 7.2–7.5).

With all teachers using the same language, it helps to make learning visible for students – they can see what dispositions you need to possess to be successful, and they are reminded on a regular basis. This was the starting point of our visible learning journey – what common language do you use in your school? How can you start implementing this into your daily teaching – make learning visible for your learners. Consistency really is key here – secondary students travel from room to room, listening to different teachers all day, no wonder their mind gets fried sometimes – have you ever shadowed a student before (PGCE and NQT teachers, I highly recommend it) you are guaranteed to feel absolutely exhausted by the end of the day.

110 *Collective teacher efficacy*

Figures 7.2-7.5 Example of primary learner attributes

Having clarity and consistency with your teachers makes the students' learning so much more structured. This also aligns itself with the Ofsted School Inspection Handbook (2021):

> The school's curriculum intent and implementation are embedded securely and consistently across the school. It is evident from what teachers do that they have a firm and common understanding of the school's curriculum intent and what it means for their practice.

High impact expectations and planning

So, how can we begin to make our teams more collaborative? Well, let's start with high impact planning: 'Planning can be done in many ways, but the most powerful is when teachers work together to develop plans, develop common understandings of what is worth teaching, collaborate on understanding their beliefs of challenge and progress, and work together to evaluate the impact of their planning on student outcomes' (Hattie, 2012, p. 41).

Again, what I often hear is, 'we would love to plan together, but we don't have the time, we've got too much to get through.' This is a valid point, the British Curriculum, in particular, is very knowledge heavy, and with only a short amount of time to get our students through so many topics and prepare them for an exam, it can become extremely overwhelming and just easier to continue to regurgitate the same resources as we have always used because we know these 'work.' As a Head of Department, my first question would be, am I happy with some of my teachers producing excellent grades each year and others not? Yes, I could put my best teachers with the top sets because I know they will stretch and challenge, and yes, I could put my stronger teachers with the lower sets because they are better at behaviour management, but what about those students in the middle? Are we doing a disservice to them? And how does this work if students are not put into sets? What this does is just provide excuses for the acceptance of stagnant teaching in the middle. The goal is to get the students a grade 5, and that is what the teacher does – and as a result, they teach to the exam and only to the exam – 'This is all they need to know to answer this question.' This is not a dig; I think we have all been guilty of this at times – just to get them through the content. It is still a success, students still achieve their target, but it becomes flatline progress. What tends to happen is we begin to accept defensive pessimism, in which we begin to make excuses for low achievement – 'oh they are a difficult cohort,' or 'these students all came up from Primary with low target grades.' As a teacher, your expectations can have a significant impact (both positively and negatively). I once heard a story about flies in a jar – they were caught in a jar which was then tightly sealed. Once in the jar, the flies tried to fly out a couple of times, but knowing they couldn't get any higher, they stopped trying. By the time the lid was finally removed, the flies had conditioned themselves that they couldn't get any higher than the seal and therefore didn't try anymore – even though the lid was off, and they were free to leave. This is the same with students – if you start with low expectations of students, creating defensive pessimism, your students will believe this too, they will not believe that they can achieve any better, and so they won't; 'students who are taught by teachers with a low sense of self-efficacy have lowered performance expectations' (Tschannen-Moran & Barr, 2004, p. 196). In 1963 there was an experiment done by Rosenthal and Jacobson in which they told the teacher that some of the students in the class had incredibly high intellect based on a Harvard test they had taken (this was made up, there was no test, and the students were picked randomly). All of the students the teacher believed were smart showed greater levels of attainment than the others. In reality, there was no difference between the students, only what was in the teacher's mind. Therefore, because of their high expectations of the students from the start, they pushed and worked hard with those students in particular. Imagine if they were told all of the students were capable of achieving amazing things!

Building in CTE can help inject a new lease of life into your department to maintain high expectations and replace outcomes (Jensen & Kelly, 2019). Donohoo (2017) believes that positive teaching behaviours that are associated with teacher efficacy are:

- Putting in greater effort and persistence with students, especially those that are struggling
- Willing to try new approaches and techniques based on researched pedagogy
- Conveying high expectations with their students
- Fostering independent learning and student autonomy
- Decreases behaviours in class that are deemed disruptive
- Have an increased commitment to their role
- A greater relationship with parents, encouraging more involvement

I have been in departments that hardly ever meet, I have been in departments that meet sporadically throughout the year, at my current school, however, the English department meets once a week. This is a good starting point to developing CTE because it allows regular contact with your team so that discussions take place. However, I know some departments struggle to make the time, and just because you are meeting each week does not mean that is enough to grow effective collective efficacy. CTE is not just about getting together and sharing resources (although I still think this is a good starting point), it goes much deeper than that. When you meet at the beginning of the year (or at the end of the year if you want to get a head start – however, your team may be a little flat at this point), start by discussing what your goal is – what is it that you want your team to achieve? Is there a percentage goal you want to hit for student attainment? Is there a certain group you particularly want to focus on? Is there a specific department weakness you need to focus on – EAL/G&T/SEN? Once you have collectively agreed on the area that you want to develop, think about your shared language for learning – for you to achieve that goal, what needs to be explicitly covered/focused on to get there? What are 'WE' collectively going to do? Just because it might not affect a certain teacher that year doesn't mean they don't have important expertise that they could share with the team. I haven't always taught a GCSE group every year, but I still get involved in the planning and moderation. I have teachers in my Media team that do not teach the BTEC, but I still get them involved in the moderation of coursework as I welcome fresh eyes and ears. Similarly, I know one of my areas of weakness is Shakespeare (I know, another bad English Teacher moment), so I welcome hearing from my colleagues – even if they are not teaching Shakespeare that year. As Donohoo (2017, p. 31) points out, 'When teachers actively participate in setting goals, they are more likely to pay attention to them as they helped in selecting them.'

Once a goal or goals have been agreed upon, next is looking at the big picture – what do students need to be able to know/achieve to be successful? This might be looking at a GCSE mark scheme or the success criteria for KS3. In Primary, I would always suggest working with the other year groups around you – what do students need to be able to do to be successful in year 6? Then work backwards, so you know what needs to be covered. What are the skills the students need to gain to be successful? As Ofsted points out in their School Inspection Handbook 2021:

> All learning builds towards an end point. Pupils are being prepared for their next stage of education, training or employment at each stage of their learning. Inspectors will consider whether pupils are ready for the next stage by the point they leave the school or provision that they attend.

Remember, however, this isn't a quick fix, and you can't change everything all at once, but you can become a 'Change Agent,' one of Hattie's other mind frames. Think about my previous chapter on self-efficacy, mastering experiences can also be done through working as a community to set goals and improve teaching and learning. As your team begins to experience success in these goals, they begin to create a momentum effect, continuing year on year to expand and grow. You begin to create professional learning communities (PLC) within your team – a strong element of CTE (Ross & Gray, 2006). So yes, it is easy to slip back into the 'I will just stick with what I already do,' but it is so much more beneficial to work collectively – yes, it might take some time at first, but you are ensuring long-term impacts, rather than short-term gains – 'view student failure as an incentive for great teacher effort' (Ross & Bruce, 2007, p. 51).

Here is a Scheme of Learning for a Year 9 Media group (Table 7.3). The weeks are broken down to show how the bigger picture will be achieved. Using the staff's expertise, the

Table 7.3 Example of a scheme of learning

Term	Unit	Big Question	Skills	What Will Be Learnt	Collective Teacher	Sources	SOLO	Assessment
Term 1 (Weeks 7–12)	Meaning/ representation	How does changes in society change our perception?	Cultural awareness	Representation – What is it and how does it change? Women in the media	CCH/LME	Posters/ magazines	**Unistructural:** Can comment on a representation	6-mark questions
			Cultural awareness	Ethnicity in the media	GHL/TBA	Posters/ magazines/ movies	**Multi-structural:** Can identify several representations	6-mark questions
			Teamwork	Comparison of representation now and then	JSH/KHU	Posters/adverts		Presentation of ideas
			Critical thinking	Comparison of posters	CCH/TBA	Poster	**Relational:** Can apply to examples and explain their effect	Written analysis
			Critical thinking	Controversial adverts	JSH/GHL	Adverts		Analysis
			Critical thinking	Analysis of OMO advert – Discussing mark scheme and success criteria	LME/KHU	OMO advert – Woman in the 50s	**Extended abstract:** Can evaluate the impact these features have on an audience	Explain how advertisements reflect the historical context in which they were created (12 mark)

resources are broken down and shared between them so that they can work collectively in producing material using SOLO Taxonomy and referring to key skills being used and taught. Following this six-week period, a review would take place to discuss the impact on student progress, and revisions can be made.

Impact cycles

I often hear the phrase 'this has always been a success for me,' be that a certain teaching style or approach – and I question what this statement actually means! How do you measure success? Is it based on results? Or is it based on the responses you get from a student? Just because a student is engaged and enjoying the work does not always necessarily mean it is having a high impact. One of the best ways to determine whether or not you are having a positive effect on your teaching and learning is by conducting your own impact cycle.

Once we had introduced visible learning to our staff, all departments and year groups were set the challenge of undergoing Impact Cycles – very similar to action research. They were asked to choose an area that they specifically wanted to focus on such as differentiation or feedback. The English department decided to focus on feedback, and after discussing this as a team, we all decided to look into different ways of providing feedback – written and verbal (Figure 7.6). To do this successfully, we needed to research different types of feedback and formative assessments.

For the first time, we actually were experimenting and trialling out new techniques – pushing ourselves out of our comfort zones and being innovative with our teaching. As I have mentioned in my previous chapter on Feedback, I had already timed myself on marking 15 Year 11 English books, it was over 2 hours! There had to be an easier, more time-efficient, and more effective way of marking and providing feedback! Now when I did this little experiment, I had to look at my practice and what I'm doing and be honest – 'Cat, this is not working!' That doesn't make me a bad teacher by admitting that what I was doing wasn't working or effective – it makes me reflective and honest. Teachers do a good job on a day-to-day basis – but you always want to challenge yourself to be better. By conducting an impact cycle, you force yourself to make a conscious effort to explore different options. If the one you are doing isn't working – find a better one and then share it!

Step 1: Determine the main area that needs focus – don't be shy of using data to inform your decision of what needs improving.
Step 2: Research, learn from others. Gather evidence to help you plan and structure your intervention. What are you going to do differently?
Step 3: Begin to implement your new approach.
Step 4: monitor the implementation and track the progress.
Step 5: Assess what the impact has been – start reviewing and planning the next steps.

The one thing to remember with impact cycles is, they are precisely that -cycles! Don't worry if when you come to assess the impact you find it isn't what you expected – review, evaluate, adapt, and start again. Educational research is pretty broad and vast, so that means

Figure 7.6 Impact cycle posters in secondary

it is often open to interpretation, so you may try something else but find yourself adapting it slightly for your specific group – that's fine! Education is complex with multiple variants involved. Maybe it might inspire you to conduct your own research and share your ideas with the teaching profession.

By completing the impact cycle as a department, you can discuss your research and findings together, share ideas and work together to build that impact. Even during the pandemic and having to move to DL doesn't stop us from evaluating our practice. In an article written by John Hattie (2020), he breaks down these key things to remember, even during COVID-19:

- Know our impact from a distance
- Learn how we as groups of teachers can evaluate, discuss, and work together
- Discover ways to enhance the collective efficacy of all (now with the parents)
- View this pandemic as an opportunity to learn more about how to work with students from afar, outside of our normal comfort zones of the classroom and school
- Engage with parents to realize we as educators have unique skills and expertise (and are happy to share them), and not get upset if students are not spending 5–6 hours every day in the belief that school at home is but a mirror of the typical school day

Micro-teaching

Now, this is probably the hardest and scariest way of really developing collective teacher efficacy – filming your lessons! I know, when someone first mentioned it to me I said, 'absolutely not!' – other than hating the sound of my own voice, I couldn't think of anything worse than watching myself back on screen. But micro-teaching, with an effect size of 0.88, is actually a really effective tool for developing teachers and building that collective teacher efficacy community within your teams. It is about creating small-scale lessons collectively with your team, recording the lesson, then analysing and reflecting through an 'under-the-microscope' session. By doing this, you allow yourself to view the lesson and discuss in a 'think aloud' way what impact was had in the classroom (Hattie & Zierer, 2018). What discussions were made and why – would you make those same discussions again? What would have a greater impact on learning? Having that dialogue with your team allows you to learn from each other and begin to implement new strategies into your own lessons.

I think COVID probably helped me be a little bit more open to this technique, as I was recording most of my lessons anyway online for students that missed the synchronous lesson so that they could play it back asynchronously. But it is not a new concept – many of the leading schools around the world have adopted this technique as common practice to help them develop professionally. There are some great examples on the OECD website that showcase this in practice. The Netherlands, in particular, uses this method as part of their teaching training, allowing teachers to support each other by reviewing lessons.

If nothing else, doing this for yourself is such a great way of really reflecting on your teaching. Besides the horror of hearing your own voice and scrutinising your dress choices for that day, you begin to see what your lesson is like in reality and how your students see you. You begin to notice and remember those times you accidentally interrupted a student or when you thought you gave them time to answer a question, but in reality, it was only like ten seconds. You can measure how much time you spend talking to your class. One thing I learnt when I watched my lesson back was that I talked when I should have been silent; often, I will set my class upon a writing task, but the whole time I would be talking to them, prompting, giving ideas, suggestions – non-stop! Watching back, I realised how distracting that actually was. Here I was thinking I was helping my students, but all I was doing was preventing them from really concentrating. I am honestly surprised one of my students didn't tell me to shut up! You also learn about your tone of voice – often, I would say something maybe a little too sarcastic or with a pitch of irritation in my voice. Now don't get me wrong, sarcasm can be fine when you have built that relationship up with students but used at the wrong time and in the wrong way could undermine your chances of building self-efficacy with your students.

Sharing these videos with your team is also useful, as they are able to see your lesson with fresh eyes – looking at it without any context. You may find that together you can work on areas and provide ideas of how to become more impactful. Remember though, this isn't about helping weaker teachers become better – even outstanding teachers can benefit from this. It is about looking reflectively at your practice and finding ways to adapt and be a change agent. Sometimes it is simply a few minor tweaks – but those tweaks can have a significant impact.

Communities of practice

As I have already mentioned, CTE is not simply getting teachers together and sharing resources but working together to seek ways of having better impactful outcomes with student attainment. Now, you can get teachers in groups and say, 'go ahead, discuss …,' however, this is not going to guarantee CTE is taking place. Have you ever been to CPD sessions where you get 5minutes to 'discuss amongst yourselves' – do you instinctively begin discussing? If you are anything like me, your first question is usually, 'so what are we doing again?' I am honestly the worst student possible – I doodle, and my mind drifts constantly. Or you may be the type that spends that time moaning, groaning, or just discussing the summer holidays until the last two minutes when you rush to put something together in case your table gets called upon to answer the question. Or are you the type of person that doesn't feel comfortable expressing your opinion, so you tend to stay quiet and go with what the majority say? Katz, Earl, and Jaafar (2009) discuss some of the issues surrounding groups which include the shirking of responsibility (I don't want to write, you write) and people are more likely to stick together than develop diversity – no one wants to be the person they outwardly disagrees with the majority at the table. Therefore, if your lead speaker at the table has a mainly negative viewpoint, then the team has a negative viewpoint. Hattie discusses how collaboration like this can often lead to 'sharing anecdotes and war stories and sharing beliefs about why or why not something might work in "my" context' (2015, p. 23). As a result of this, these types of group gatherings and discussions 'can be a grand waste of time' (Fullan & Quinn, 2016, p. 13).

However, with the right structure and guidance, teams can be extremely effective for developing CTE and improving teaching and learning. I have come across many different variations of these types of teams, whether they are known as PLC, Communities of Practice (CoP), or Triads, and they all have the same common goals of:

- focusing on improving student learning
- taking collective responsibility and understanding, we are all responsible for students learning
- continuous improvements
- being evidence-driven

Just before COVID-19 hit us and we moved to distant learning, I had begun working with our Teaching and Learning Practitioners (TLPs), who had been specifically picked due to their excellence in different aspects of teaching and learning. As a group, we discussed areas in our teaching and learning we felt we needed even more development on (see, even the best teachers want to improve). Some said they wanted to develop their ability to work with EAL students, others wanted to focus on AG&T and some on improving feedback. So, we created our first T&L triads or CoPs (Community of Practice).

Research into CoPs has shown both short-term and long-term values of using these in your organisation. The short term allows you to focus on specific challenges you might be currently facing in school, you can use your experts already on the ground to help build and lead the CoP, it builds confidence as it is teachers leading other teachers, staff enjoy being a part of change, especially when they know they are working towards meaningful work and have that shared vision. And in the long term, this builds long-term personal development of staff, you can then enhance your reputation that your staff are innovative and keeping up to date with current evidence-based research. However, I think it is important to note that putting together a CoP where teachers can collaborate and gain all these positives can only work if it has a biased towards action. While it feels good to chat with a group of colleagues and share ideas and research, it has to then move from the theoretical into actual action for progress to occur. This is something we are really proud of achieving at my current school.

With my visible learning CoP, I have asked my team to evaluate their departments' needs and pick an area that needs developing, such as feedback or differentiation. They will then work together to research new ways to improve this area before putting together an action plan to begin implementing their research to action ideas into their lessons. Building their self-efficacy and confidence in the classroom encourages them to become more innovative and experimental. They can then evaluate their impact, calculate their effect sizes and analyse the impact they have had on their students. This is only possible if and when the research made has been put into action and evaluated. Once this is successfully achieved, we are then able to utilise our CoP experts, encouraging them to share their success with the rest of our staff members through our bespoke CPD so that others can also adopt these techniques and use them in their own teaching.

So, to summarise, encourage collective teacher efficacy, whether this is a whole school focus or a department focus. Be evaluative and identify the areas that need improvement or development. Use evidence-based research to gather ideas to share amongst your team. Turn your researched knowledge into action by trying out new techniques in your lessons through your impact cycle and evaluate the impact it has had on teaching and learning. If no impact, tweak/revise/try again. Learning never stops – don't give up, have that growth mindset to keep you searching to be collectively better.

Professional development

The development of teachers is important to ensure teaching and learning doesn't become stagnant. Education is constantly changing, and new research is constantly being introduced and reviewed, so it makes sense to stay on top of these changes and ensure your staff have access to the most up-to-date methods. Research-informed information is so important, as you have the evidence to back up the impact – by ignoring these tried and tested techniques could leave teachers falling behind in knowledge and pedagogy. With an effect size of 0.62, we know it has the potential to be successful in developing staff – however it has many variant factors meaning if you are going to provide professional development, make sure it is, again, effective. Sometimes there is the need to get external expertise, especially in subject-specific areas, but professional development can also take place in-house through offering bespoke CPD.

We began providing bespoke CPD to our staff by asking them specifically what areas they felt they needed support in. There is nothing more annoying than having to sit in a CPD session for an hour that isn't targeted at you – teacher time is precious at the best of times, so it is important it is used efficiently. By giving staff options, they were able to have more autonomy over their own professional development. Using our TLPs, we could get our 'experts' to lead on the sessions, providing research, examples, and tasks for staff to try out themselves. One of the sessions we ran had two parts to it, this first was the initial session to present on the research and examples of the topic with a task for staff to go away and try and do – be that embed a technique into their lesson, or research further – then following a few weeks we met again to discuss our findings, what worked, what didn't and where we could go next with it. We also always send out a questionnaire following these bespoke CPDs to get feedback from staff – sometimes they are very positive, sometimes we are given constructive criticism – all help us plan and revise. Like everything else, feedback is key – feedback can allow you to know how to improve your bespoke CPD so that you are constantly evaluating and revisiting, but it is also important to give teachers concrete goals to work towards so that they can give themselves self-regulatory feedback.

Social media

I love the coming together of the education profession on social media – I have been blogging my ideas since 2013, but often I will go on to Twitter or Instagram and see so many wonderful ideas that inspire me to try something new. Just starting conversations on there and hearing different people's experiences and opinions when it comes to education, especially listening to all the different approaches all around the world. What I have loved seeing this summer is how many teachers out there are beginning to be more active with their reading and researching – sharing their favourite books and discussing how it has helped them grow as a professional. Through these platforms, I have come across some amazing and inspirational people and their podcasts. Here are my top five podcasts and Twitter handles:

1. Teachers Talk Radio – @TTRadio2021
2. @KateJones_Teach
3. Naylor's Natter Podcast – @pna1977
4. @DylanWiliam
5. LearnLiveUAE Podcast

Chapter Summary

- Share best practice with other members of staff.
- Develop a trial and error approach within teams.
- Use department 'experts' to set high expectations and ensure all learning is excellent with high impact.
- Encourage impact cycles as a department in order to implement and monitor teaching strategies.
- Record lessons in order to be reflective and evaluate teaching and learning in practice.
- Work in groups to ensure that impact is taking place.

So, what does an 'outstanding' teacher do?

They actively research and share ideas with their colleagues, working together to ensure they collectively have a stronger impact on their students' learning. Collectively using impact cycles to implement and monitor effective teaching strategies and sharing best practice. They work closely with the 'experts' to develop their own teaching and learning and understand that learning never ends.

References

Donohoo, J. (2017). *Collective efficacy: How educators' beliefs impact student learning*. Thousand Oaks, CA: Corwin.

Eells, R. J. (2011). *Loyola eCommons meta-analysis of the relationship between collective teacher efficacy and student achievement recommended citation*. https://ecommons.luc.edu/cgi/viewcontent.cgi?article=1132&context=luc_diss

Fullan, M., & Quinn, J. (2016). *Coherence the right drivers in action for schools, districts, and systems*. Thousand Oaks, CA: Corwin.

Georgiou, S., Christou, C., Stavrinides, P., & Panaoura, G. (2002). Teacher attributions of student failure and teacher behavior toward the failing student. *Psychology in the Schools, 39*(5), 583–595.

Hargreaves, A., & Fullan, M. (2012). *Professional capital: Transforming teaching in every school*. New York, NY: Teachers' College Press.

Hattie, J. (2020). *Visible learning effect sizes when schools are closed: What matters and what does not*. https://opsoa.org/application/files/2215/8689/0389/Infuences-during-Corona-JH-article.pdf

Hattie, J. (2012). *Visible learning for teachers: Maximizing impact on learning*. London: Routledge.

Hattie, J. (2015). *What works best in education: The politics of collaborative expertise*. London: Pearson International.

Hattie, J., & Zierer, K. (2018). *Ten mindframes for visible learning: Teaching for success*. Abingdon, Oxon: Routledge.

Jensen, T., & Kelly, C. (2019, June 4). *Collective teacher efficacy*. Retrieved from Teaching Channel website. https://www.teachingchannel.com/blog/collective-teacher-efficacy

Kanter, R. (2006). *Confidence: How winning streaks and losing streaks begin & end*. New York: Three Rivers Press.

Katz, S., Earl, L. M., & Jaafar, S. B.(2009). *Building and connecting learning communities: The power of networks for school improvement*. Thousand Oaks, CA: Corwin.

Ofsted. (2021). *School inspection handbook*. Retrieved from GOV.UK website. https://www.gov.uk/government/publications/school-inspection-handbook-eif/school-inspection-handbook

Ross, J. A., & Bruce, C. (2007). Professional development effects on teacher efficacy: Results of randomized field trial. *Journal of Educational Research, 101*(1), 50-60.

Ross, J. A., & Gray, P. (2006). Transformational leadership and teacher commitment to organizational values: The mediating effects of collective teacher efficacy. *School Effectiveness and School Improvement, 17*(2), 179-199.

Tschannen-Moran, M., & Barr, M. (2004). Fostering student learning: The relationship of collective teacher efficacy and student achievement. *Leadership and Policy in Schools, 3*(3), 189-209.

UNESCO. (2020, September 23). *How teachers are leading efforts to ensure learning never stops during COVID-19 education disruption*. Retrieved from UNESCO website. https://en.unesco.org/news/how-teachers-are-leading-efforts-ensure-learning-never-stops-during-covid-19-education

Index

Note: Page numbers in *italics* refers to Figures, and pages in **bold** refer to Tables.

action research 2, 4, 5, 8, 114
Akınoğlu, O. 54
Armstrong, P. 13
Arnett, J. 41
assessment 17, 47, **55**, 59-60, **65**-66, **113**; and assessment for learning (AFL) **55**, 60, 73-74
autonomy 16, 19, 51, 111, 119

Baker, L. 44
Bandura, A. 9, 77-78, 84-86, 100, 103
Barr, M. 111
Beattie, S. 91
Beere, J. 62
Benson, L. 94; *see also* EPOCH
Betts, G.H. 32
Biggs, J. 5, 12, 16
Blackweell, L.S. 92
Bloom's Taxonomy 12, *13*, 16, 19,
brain training 8
Brandt, R. 4
Brooks, C. 71
Butler, R. 58

Caviglioli, O. 36
challenge 2, 6-7, 9, 17, 19, 26, 32-36, 46, **50**, 53, **55**, 56, 73, 77, 79, 89, 91, 108, 110-111, 114
Clarke, S. 8, 18, 48, 58, 72
closed question 6, 32-33; *see also* questioning
cognition **42**, 93; cognitive acceleration 8, 46; cognitive apprenticeship 8, 49, **50**, 56; cognitive development 40-41, 46-47, 56; and cognitive load theory 8, 54; meta-cognitive ability 78

collective language for learning 10, 108
collective teacher efficacy 2, **4**, 10, 103-120
Collis, K.F. 5, 12
communities of practice (COPs) 10, 116-118
competing commitments 80-81
concrete operational 7, 41, **42**, 56
Covington, M.V. 80, 84
critical thinking 7, 28-30, 38, 54, **113**

dialogue 6, 7, 26, 31-34, 38, 46, 116
differentiation 6, 13, 15, 17, 21, **55**, 114, 118
DIRT **50**, 62-63, 65, 71, 84
Dinham, S. 74
Dinther, M.V. 95
Dockterman, D. 33
Donohoo, J. 103, 105, 108, 111-112
Duckworth, A. 90, 95
Dweck, C. 9, 78, 81, 91

Eagly, A.H. 90
EAL 14-16, 18, 19, 112, 118
Ebbinghaus, H. 8, 42-43, *44*, 48
EBI **50**, 71
Education Endowment Foundation (EEF) 49, 72
Education Inspection Framework 59, 61
Eells, R.J. 104
effect sizes *3*, 6, 8, 26, 58, 85, **104**, 116, 119
efficacy 103, 105, 108; collective efficacy 2, **4**, 10, 89, 103-**104**, 106, 108, 112, 116, 118; self-efficacy 10, 33, 65, 77-79, *80*, 81, 84-85, 90-**93**, 95, 97-**99**, 100, 103, 105; *see also* Bandura
Elliot, V. 72

emotional and physiological states 10, 93, 103
environment 2-3, 38, 46, **50**, 53, 77, 89, 103, **104**
EPOCH 94-95, 100
Eva, A. 85
Extended Abstract 5, 12, **14**, 16, 20-21, 41, **42**, 81-82, **113**; see also SOLO

Faircloth, E. 98
feedback 1, 7, **4**, 8-9, 17, 32, 37, 47, 58-59, **60**, 60-67, **68**, 69-75; feedback mats 70; feed-forward 64; group feedback 69; oral feedback **60**; peer feedback **60**, 74; process-based 62; self-regulatory 66; task-based 60-61; teacher feedback 71; verbal feedback 9, **55**, 60, 72-74; whole class feedback 69, 73; written feedback 72-73
Fixed mindsets 9, 32-33, 89, 91-92, 105; see also mindsets; Growth mindsets
flipped learning, 8, **50**, 53-54, **55**
Fogg, B.J. 96
Forgetting Curve, 8, 42, 44, 48; see also Ebbinghaus, H.
formal operational 7, 41, **42**, 46-47, 53, 56; see also Piaget
Fullan, M. 108, 117

Gates, B. 1
Gibson, D.E. 86
Griffin, M. 95, 98-99; see also VESPA
Growth mindset 9, 33, 89, 91-92, 100, 104-105, 118; see also mindsets; fixed mindsets

Halvorson, H. 62
Hargreaves, A. 108
Hattie, J. 2-4, 6-8, 18, 26, 46, 48, 58-59, 71-72, 85, 103-106, **104**, **107**, 110, 112, 116-117; see also effect sizes; impact cycles; visible learning
high expectations 7, 34, 36-37, 87, **107**, 111, 120
high impact planning 10, 110
higher-order thinking 13, 19, 45, 47
Hook, P. 16-17, 80; see also SOLO
Huppert, F.A. 95

impact cycles 2, 10, 114-*115*, 118, 120; see also effect sizes; Hattie, J.; visible learning
IRE 32, 62

James, I.A. 27
Jensen, T. 111
Jerusalem, M. 98-99; see also efficacy
Jones 47, 60, 69, 119; see also retrieval practice

Kanter, R. 105
Kapur, M. 82
Karpicke, J. 47
Katz, S. 117
Kegan, R. 80
Kern, M. 94; see also EPOCH
Kraft, M.A. 2

Lahey, J. 30, 93
Launier, R. 84
Lazarus, R.S. 84
Lea, K. 86
learner characteristics 108
Learning Pit 79; see also Nottingham
learning objectives (LO) 5-6, 9, 12, 17-18, *20*, 20-21, 59
Lemov, D. 37-38
Leroy, N. 92
Levin, B.B. 4
Lovell, O. 54

McCrindle, M. 10
McGill, R. 72-73
McNeill, L. 17
meta-analysis 3; see also Hattie, J.; visible learning
metacognition 7-9, 40-42, 44; see also cognition
Meyer, W. 91
Michael, J. 54
Millar, S. 46
mindframes 105
mindsets 77, 81, 84, 89-92, **93**, 95, 98, 100; see also Fixed Mindsets; Growth Mindsets
modelling 8-9, 12, 28, 34, 38, 46, 49-**50**, 51-52, 56, **60**, 70, 73, 85-87, *87*, 88, 90, 100
Morris, B.J. 92
multi-structural *14*, 15-16, 19, 21, **60**, *81-82*; see also SOLO
Murre, J.M.J. 48

Nottingham 79; see also Learning Pit

Oakes, S. 95, 98-99; *see also* VESPA
O'Dowd, D.K. 54
OECD 34, 116
Ofsted 59, 61-62, 94, 110, 112
open question 28
Orlando, J.D. 62

Pajares, F. 93
Papay, J.P. 2
Pearson, J.A. 89
pedagogy 3-4, 11, 111, 119
performance outcomes 9, 78, 91; *see also* Bandura
PERMA 94; *see also* Seligman, M.
perseverance 78, 89-90, 92, 94, 97, 100
persuasion 9, 90, 91-92, 100, 103; *see also* Bandura; efficacy, self-efficacy
Piaget 7, 40-42, **42**, 46
plenary 15, 23, **68**
preoperational 7, 41, **42**; *see also* Piaget
pre-structural, 5, *14*, 17, 20, 79, *81-82*; *see also* SOLO
process-based 8, 62; *see also* feedback

questioning (question) 1, 4-9, *13*, 15, 21, 26-27, **27**, **28**, 28-38, 44, 47, 49, **50**, 51-53, **55**, 56, **60**, 62, 64-65, **68**, 69, 73-74, 84, 86, 103, 105, 111, **113**, 114, 116-117; *see also* closed question; open question; Socratic
Quigley, A. 49, 59, **60**

reassessment contract **65**, 84
reflection 4, 6, 17, *24*, 27, **50**, **55**, 62, 65, 84, 106; *see also* DIRT
relational 5, *14*, 15-16, 19, 21, 36, 41, **42**, **60**, *81-82*, **113**; *see also* SOLO
Renton, M. 6, 31-32, 34; *see also* questioning
resilience 63, *67*, 77-78, 89, 92, 94, 97, 100, 108-109
retrieval practice 8, 15, 47-48, **50**, 56, 61, 73, 108; *see also* Ebbinghaus, H.; Jones
Rice, J.K. 1
Riches, A. 69
Ross, J.A. 112

Sadler, R. 17, 58, 62
scaffolding 41, **50**-52, **60**, 88-*89*

Schwarzer, R. 98-99; *see also* Efficacy
self-regulation **4**-5, 16-17, 59, 66-**68**, 98
Seligman, M. 94; *see also* PERMA
sensorimotor 7, 40, **42**, 56; *see also* Piaget
Shayer, M. 46-47
Sherrington, T. 36, 43
Shrestha, P. 48
SMART targets *67*
Socratic 6-7, 26-28, **27**, 30, 38, **50**; seminars 6, **28**-**29**, 30-31; *see also* questioning
SOLO 5-6, 8, 12-13, *14*, 16-25, 33, 36, **42**, **50**, **55**, **60**, 67, 71, 80-81, *81*, *82*, 106, **113**-114; *see also* Hook, P.
Steinberg, E.A. 94; *see also* EPOCH
Stevens-Fulbrook, P. 42, 88
success criteria 5, 17, *24*, **28**, **50**, 59, **60**, 62, **65**, **68**, 71, 87-*88*, 112-**113**

Tomsett, J. 8, 49
Tschannen-Moran, M. 111

Undercover Classroom 90
UNESCO 106

Van der Stel, M. 45
VESPA 10, 95-96, 98
vicarious experiences 9, 84, 92, 100; *see also* Bandura; efficacy
visible learning 2-4, 40, 71, 105-106, 109, 114, 118; *see also* Hattie, J.
Vygotsky, L. 7, 40, 88

Wangwongwiroj, T. 91-93
Watanabe-Crockett, L. 29-31, 54; *see also* questioning
Wiliam, D. 5, 17, 59-60
Willingham, D. T. 42, 44, 73
Wolfe, P. 4

Yasri, P. 91-93
Yeager, D.S. 91

Zakrzewski, V. 80
Zentall, S.R. 92
zonal marking, 73-74; *see also* Vygotsky, L.

For Product Safety Concerns and Information please contact our EU
representative GPSR@taylorandfrancis.com
Taylor & Francis Verlag GmbH, Kaufingerstraße 24, 80331 München, Germany

www.ingramcontent.com/pod-product-compliance
Lightning Source LLC
Chambersburg PA
CBHW082101230426
43670CB00017B/2921